TO MEND A Broken HEART

NATIONAL BESTSELLING AUTHOR

MYUNIQUE C. GREEN

Copyright © 2025 by Myunique C. Green

All rights reserved. This book or any portion thereof may not be reproduced or used in any manner whatsoever without the express written permission of the publisher except for the use of brief quotations in a book review. To protect the privacy of parties involved some names have been changed.

First publication in 2018.

ISBN: 978-1-105-95371-2

MyuniqueGreen.com

Snapchat @ CeCe_Major
Instagram @ *cmajor*_

Unless otherwise noted, scriptures are quoted from *New World Translation of the Holy Scriptures,* available for free download from JW.org

Distributed by iWriteBooks Publishing

"Heartbreaking as it is inspiring. The things that happened to Myunique are real. I love how she kept real to the events that happened no matter how horrifying they are." -The Booksnake Etc.

"It's real and it's raw." -Bookish Deer

"To Mend a Broken Heart by Myunique C. Green is the most moving memoir I have ever come across. By writing about her tragedies, low self-esteem, and insecurities, the author has reassured her readers that there is hope. Her faith saved her, and it can actually save so many of us."- Readers Favorite

"I am simply amazed and inspired by this (true) story from Myunique. It's truly a rare thing for an author to have the strength to write in such a raw and honest way. An absolute must read for those who seek personal growth or those trying to heal from their past experiences." -Taya DeVere, author of Between Two Doors

CONNECT WITH MYUNIQUE

Amazon   Goodreads   Blog

For the many nights that you spent up bothering me while I finished—this one is still for you Nysan.

Author's Notes

My story isn't all bad.

At least that's what I will keep telling myself so that I can make it through. I've said for years that I'm just a girl with a story to tell and no one to listen.

In the beginning, I wanted my story to be in chronological order; but the thing about that is, you'd have to sit through so many fuzzy memories. Instead, I'm going to write the memories as they come, and hopefully by the end you'll see the whole picture.

Although there is a chapter to correspond with every year of my life so far, it isn't written that way.

I pulled twenty-six moments.

Twenty-six experiences that have shaped me and brought me to this place of acceptance.

Going forward, I want to take the time out to thank the people who have meant so much to me through this journey. The people that were subjected to hear this story repeatedly just so I could get the tone right.

I can never thank those people enough.

My most heartfelt appreciation must go to my best friend who has been sticking with me on some of my worst days, and still looks at me with the same twinkle whenever I enter the room. So many days are easier when you're around. I must admit that.

I'd also like to say that the woman I am now cares very little about hurt feelings. I've been the poster child for self-pity and avoiding saying what's really on my mind for far too long. I know some people in my family are going to be upset.

Some may cry.

Some may say that I should have just kept this all bottled inside until I couldn't hold on to it any longer.

They're okay to feel how they want to.

As for me, I refuse to be an active volcano waiting to blow my top.

The funny thing is that it was the screams that brought me to this conclusion. It was the panic attacks, the inability to sleep and the horrible tension headaches that made me realize that I've had enough of holding it all in.

Every scream was for the little girl inside.

Every tear.

Every time I said, "I'm fine" just so that people would be okay with going back to treating me as if I were invisible.

I thought about naming this The Invisible Girl, and as you read, you'll know why. But as I sat and examined the memories and emotional scars, I knew that they weren't the makings of someone who was invisible, but of a girl who was just broken.

In more ways than one.

All Over the Place

I don't think I've ever quite felt this way about someone before. It's so easy for me to lose myself in thoughts about the way he laughs, how he walks, with that undeniable swagger. Sometimes I find myself just thinking about the soft brown of his eyes and the way that he would look at me when we were having good days.

There were so many good days.

I would go so far as to say that what happened between us was my fault—that somehow, I brought the pain I now feel upon myself. But I know that would be a lie. It would only serve to further his agenda of making me feel like the culprit in everything that I do.

So, why am I writing about him? Why have I been thinking about him so often? He's like a walking nightmare can't escape.

My own personal version of Hell.

With that said, I have to do what I do best—I must write about it.

Get it out of my system before I lose myself to the darkness that continues to bud inside of my heart. Spreading like a fatal disease.

I just chuckled out loud a little bit.

Have you ever been equal parts damaged and repaired?

One part of you feeling so complete as if you can face anything and the other side just hanging on to remind you that this could be the end.

I feel like that all the time.

Even more so now that I have cut all ties with the one I believed was the love of my life for so long. The funny thing is, I can't bring myself to hate him for all the self-torment he subjected me to. But then again, I can't really hate anyone for doing that to me.

I've done a lot of the damage to myself.

Before you write me off as just another professional victim, just allow me to tell my side of the story. Perhaps this is the most honest I've been in a long time. I'm not going to expect people to understand—but I hope they do. I hope you get it. Even if you don't, I hope you can pass it on to someone who will.

A Little Better

I'm going to tell you the truth because I have no reason to lie.

My heart is broken.

It was just fragile at first, but now it's completely in pieces on the floor—and where's the glue when you need it? For quite some time I've lived in this world where love doesn't dwell. The kind of world that's dark and gritty like an old, black and white murder-mystery movie. It's hard to say when it first started; maybe it was growing up and seeing so many bad things happen to good people. Maybe it began to build in me as I would constantly witness my mother being beaten bloody every other day.

But she loved him so much.

Maybe that was the thing that made me decide that love just didn't exist, and if it did, it sure had dire consequences.

You can call me whatever you want for that.

For the most part, I've just been the weird kid all my life. But for some reason, everyone seemed to love me. Was it due to everyone realizing that my home situation was less than ideal? Perhaps. When I would go to school, so many people took pity on me.

Because I'm such a pretty girl, they said.

And smart too.

They all knew something that I didn't. Something that I was blinded from seeing.

I'm sorry if it feels like I'm jumping all over the place, I just want to write the words as I feel them bleeding from this old heart of mine.

It still aches.

But I'm talking about the little girl. That miniature version of me was relentlessly pitied. Only I didn't see the attention as empathy.

Now that I look back through my little girl eyes, I see everything for what it was. All the sad looks and the whispers to other teachers that I couldn't comprehend. It all makes sense now—well, mostly.

See, I've lived in an emotionless world. I learned a long time ago that when you feel things, it only makes it hard to do anything.

So, I watched.

I listened.

I retreated so far into myself that I have a positive relationship with the voices in my head that tend to sound like other people.

People that I like.

People I can relate to.

People who understand.

If I'm going to be completely honest here, I have regular conversations with myself, even as an adult. I've been led to believe that it's healthy too. The voices didn't go away, even after I built positive relationships with people outside of myself. I wish it were true that they did. But that, my friends, would be a lie.

Often when I think of myself as a kid, I go back to the times after my mother left my first stepfather. Those memories are a little better. I was a little older. It's the repressing of those memories back then that have helped me to move forward. But in doing so, I think I may have inhibited myself—those should come out too.

Safe

Now that I've kind of set the scene, let's bring out the five-year-old girl first. I yearn to say that things were ideal. That life was just what you would imagine for a young girl just beginning her tender years.

They were not.

It's funny for me to think that I was once a happy baby. One so full of life.

I can only really remember one main thing about that girl—she wanted her mother's love. There wasn't much that she wouldn't do to get it. But as life would have it, her mother was busy giving away all the love that was meant for her to someone else. Someone who didn't deserve it.

I remember waking up in the middle of the night after a nightmare. The only thing on my mind was that if I could get into bed with my mommy everything would be okay. I would be safe. The problem wasn't making it to the bed though—I did that. The difficulty was staying in the bed.

I don't think I've ever been shoved out of a bed so fast.

That small child slept under their bed that night, too afraid to go back to the shared room with her siblings. It wasn't the last time she cuddled under their bed, silently sobbing in the dark. In fact, there were a couple of times they had sex right on top of the bed as she lay under it. The springs would press so firmly against her face.

But she couldn't make a sound.

Couldn't leave.

A beating would have swiftly followed if she had even attempted to roll from beneath the bed.

That's where her self-image began to deteriorate.

That's when she felt invisible.

As if nothing or no one in this world cared. They were all willing to let the monsters get her, and no one would miss her once they did.

If I could talk to that little girl now, I would tell her not to cry. That girl would be wrapped tightly in my arms as I carried her back to that room and tucked her beneath the blanket.

I'm not sure what kept me under that bed at night and the nights to follow. Perhaps it had something to do with the security that came from just being near her. The childish belief that the monsters couldn't see me if I were under there, in earshot of my mommy.

It's apparent to me that it was around this time I was cursed with invisibility; something that is not as fun as they make it out to be in the movies.

At least not when you want to be seen.

In the beginning, I took my invisibility in stride, I learned when and what I could get away with quickly–which wasn't much. Most of the time, I was contemplating how to avoid getting a beating. Those were some of my worst days. The only time things started to seem like they could possibly get better, was when I was away from all of them.

Move Mountains

I spent a lot of time running away from home. Honestly, I don't remember what made me start running, but I would just wonder off in search of something—anything.

It didn't matter where I was or who I was with, if at any point I was given the opportunity to break out, that's exactly what I was doing.

There was this one time that I was staying with a family friend. It was supposed to just be for a night, but it ended up dragging on longer than I expected. During my stay there, I came to find out that a woman I would much rather stay with lived in the same apartments.

It didn't take me long to plan my escape.

I waited until everyone was good and sleep. The television had shut off for the night (back in my day, TV would just go off air at a certain time) and it was pitch black in the whole house—except for the grey blur that illuminated from the TV screen. I listened for a moment, listening for the sound that someone may be awake in the living room. My little legs were shaking when I got up and made my way into the dark room, doing my best to be as quiet as I could.

I'd almost made it to the door when my foot caught underneath someone and I crashed onto the floor, toppling over that person. With my heart racing and my head spinning, I ran back into the room and waited for the person to get up from the floor and come into the room to discipline me. Ladies and gentlemen, I was always in constant fear of being beaten.

But nothing happened.

Soon, I listened for the snores again and upon determining that the coast was clear, I got up from the bed once again and made my way into the living room. This time, I was aware of the man lying in the middle of the floor, so I carefully stepped over him.

The next obstacle was opening the door. How could I do it without anyone hearing anything? I fumbled around in the dark for a long time, before finally building up enough courage to twist it and open the door.

The night air was warm and humid. All I wore was an oversized, white t-shirt and underwear.

I'd left the door to the apartment open because I was too afraid to close it behind me. I still remember the smell of the pool that the apartment was directly in front of. It glistened as I walked past it, determined to find where my relative was.

I may have wandered out there for hours. My feet were hurting and I was just walking around in countless circles looking for the door with the white circle on it.

I had walked so long I forgot where the apartment I was staying at was located. When I was ready to give up and sleep on the stairs somewhere—and I think I did sit down on the steps from pure exhaustion—I heard my name ring out of the darkness.

My cousin found me sitting on the stairs, face resting inside the palms of my tiny hands, and took me to his house. I don't think I've ever been quite excited to see him to this day. I didn't understand what my cousin was doing outside in the middle of the night back then, but I was glad he was.

That night, I slept under the warmth of the woman who felt more like a mother than mine ever did. I've suppressed that memory for about three years now.

It makes me feel.

That woman was so good to me and she was biologically just my cousin. But she took me in, made me feel loved, carried me with her wherever she went. I loved her so much. It hurts the worse now that she's gone to rest, and I'm left with the memories of that little girl who would move mountains to be wrapped in her embrace one more time.

What saddens me the most is the fact that she only saw me grow up to be just an *okay* adult. I say that because I wasn't in-and-out of jail or constantly in getting in trouble. I just flew under the radar on a lot of things.

When it comes to Mama Clara, I'm either feeling nothing at all, or everything all at once. It's a pain that I can't think about too long, and I don't think I'll ever outgrow that.

I guess I'm supposed to either.

No, I'm not still grieving, but she took a piece of me with her, and I can't get that back until I see her again. So, I guess you can say that I'm in a constant state of waiting.

Waiting to see her smile again.

Waiting to hear her say my name and do that full-belly laugh that brought me so much comfort.

Just as I suspected.

I'm crying now.

That's okay though, because these are the kind of tears that I'm alright with. I know that these sorts of tears are out of my control as long as I can't pick up the phone to call and talk to her.

Called My Bluff

I remember the first day of kindergarten like it was twenty years ago. Therefore, it mostly includes choppy pieces of a story that are hazy recollections at best.

When I arrived to class, there were so many faces. So many children and bright colors. My name was already written on the desk, and I remember endlessly tracing it for most of the day with my finger.

My teachers were both male and female, and by the third day of school, they both took turns redirecting me constantly. Even on days when I thought I was having a good day, something would always happen that would make me cross out one of my conduct stickers on the wall.

I hated kindergarten.

One thing I did like about it though, was that if you lost a tooth, you received a lollipop. When I discovered that little treasure, I think I may have lost a tooth every other week. How? I found this piece of gravel that looked exactly like a tooth. I used it so frequently that eventually my teachers just gave me a lollipop if I promised to behave.

The thing is, I don't think I was a bad kid, and at this point, I really feel like my teacher hated me.

So, Ms. Flakes, if you just so happen to read this one day, you should know that I thought you were the worst teacher in the world. I could never do any right in your eyes, and you made me hate coming to school every day.

The good news is, that my teachers got better as I got older. In first grade, I loved my teacher very much and I can't remember for the life of me her name. By that time, I had already changed schools and moved into the house that eventually became known as a Hell House.

I may have gotten some of my worst beatings there.

It was around the time of first grade that I began to learn the art of manipulation. There's something about being in physical and mental torment that makes you, I don't know, want to get out of it.

We changed schools a lot though, so I'm not entirely surprised that I don't remember most of the names of my teachers. The only reason I could pull my kindergartens teacher name out of a dusty, old hat is because I disliked her so much.

I remember being enrolled at the same school as my younger cousin at Tidwell Elementary, that school isn't around anymore because they tore it down. Undoubtedly due to the severe state of disrepair it was in. If there was ever a time I felt the sting of my poverty, it was when I was in that school. Even at seven, you know that a school is supposed to have working air conditioning and no leaks in the roof.

That's beside the point.

When my cousin and I were at the school together, it gave me a sense of relief. I loved my cousin—especially because she was naïve and took my word for everything since I was older.

We laugh about it now.

I think I conned her out of her lunch money every day until I left that raggedy school. Sometimes I would tell her that because I had five pennies and she only had four quarters, I had more money than she did; therefore, we should trade so that she would have more money than me.

I don't think she'll ever let me forget it either.

We grew up to be the best of cousins. Although a little rocky at first. By rocky, I mean she punched me in the eye one time because I didn't know how to shut my mouth.

I dared her, thinking she wouldn't do it.

She called my bluff.

That was my first black eye.

It was strange how my family worked to make each other tougher—or maybe that's the way families are supposed to treat each other. I had interesting times with my cousins, to say the least.

We would simulate a whooping, essentially, we were taking turns hitting each other, trying to prepare for the next one. The goal was not to cry anymore. We figured that if we could train ourselves not to feel it, that would make getting a whooping a lot easier to bear.

That method never worked. We were always caught by surprise, and eventually my mother graduated from a belt to one of those black cable cords.

One morning when I was restarting the third grade—yes, you saw it right—I decided to skip the first day.

Two of my cousins, who were in different school districts, had come over and walked us to school, and convinced me that since I was moving anyways, I should ditch it all together. I listened to them, and spent the day roaming around the neighborhood, just doing nothing.

That was a fun day, although it ended with all of us getting in trouble. That was alright though, we had our fun while it lasted. Come to think of it, I got into a lot of trouble with my cousins too, but it oddly always seemed worth it.

Go to Bed

My mother went through a period in her life where these random guys would pop around. I was then too young to understand what exactly was going on, but I do remember their faces. I remember trying to comprehend why they were around in the first place.

I still wanted my mommy's love and attention. The fact that she constantly gave it away to outsiders did a number on my self-esteem.

There was this one guy that I just couldn't stand. He was mean and honestly wanted nothing to do with kids. See, by the time he came around, there were three of us. This stage of my life was interesting.

I don't know if the man's real name was Joe, but that's what he called himself. His skin was bronze and his hair was black with curls just on the top. The accent he spoke with always made me uncomfortable and I believe it was because he said he was from Australia. One time that man told us he wrestled and ate alligators. None of which I can look back and genuinely believe.

When Joe was around, we were neither to be seen or heard. It would have to be like there were no kids in the house at all. Luckily, he only came around at night, so it wasn't hard to just go to bed.

There were no more beatings though.

No more walking on eggshells because the slightest mistake could trigger someone's rage.

What took the place of the beatings was the fact that Anthony, a middle school kid that lived across the way in our duplex homes, wanted to have sex with me. I was about eight years old. He hounded me every day when he got home from school. He would expose himself to me, try to grab and kiss me. I spent most of the time while living in those apartments trying to shove him off.

One day, while playing outside, he cornered me. It wasn't just him this time though, he had brought a friend along with him.

They chased me down.

Once captured, I was pinned to the ground while Anthony grabbed all over my body with one hand, while covering my mouth with the other. All I could hear is the pounding of my heart as it beat in my ears. I struggled myself into exhaustion. Then, someone caught them, ran them away from me. Every day after that I never felt safe. I couldn't quite explain exactly what happened to anyone and if I said anything, no one would have believed me.

That boy never actually raped me.

But he always got close.

Too close.

There may be something that was going on in their house that no one knew as well. The boy had a sister, her name was Kimberly, and she bullied me constantly. I've only been spit on a few times in my life, and every time it was from her mouth. As I think about it, knowing what I know now, the problem was probably much deeper than them and I honestly hope that they're out there doing okay for themselves.

I don't wish evil on anyone.

Like them though, I do believe that I will pay for the things that I have done. Even if I didn't know any better.

I was so angry. Full of rage and aggression.

I also had no one to turn to.

Nobody taught me how to cope. I feel as though I was ultimately just thrown to the wolves and left alone to fend for myself.

Natural Selection.

That may have made me somewhat of a bully. I can recall a specific time that my anger got the best of me when a small boy that lived in the duplex next to us came over. I think my mom was supposed to be babysitting, but one of her men called and she was out of the door like a rocket.

I remember so vividly beating that boy up just to see him cry. To stare into his eyes as they filled with tears and displayed the hopelessness that I felt on the inside. The only thing that made me stop was the fact that the boy had on a red shirt, and as I was jostling him around, the collar of his shirt flew over his mouth; I thought I had made him bleed. I took a deep breath, stood up straight, dragged him across the floor by his arm, threw him across the bed, and told him to go to sleep. Thinking of the way he must have felt almost brings tears to my eyes.

I feel bad about it—I really do.

This is the first time I have thought about all of this in over a decade. It just seems like a distant dream; I couldn't have possibly behaved that way. But I did. I can't even remember the kids name and odds are he was too young to remember.

We did not stay in that duplex for very long. The first stepfather found out where we lived and started to come around again. After that, we were back under his oppressive wing.

Fast forward a little bit and you have us moving to a shelter. For the most part, I spent a lot of time being confused about why we had to live there in the first place, but once we were there, I actually came to like it.

My experience in the shelter was different. We did not really come with many clothes, but we were always clean.

School for us was the YMCA, maybe because we were only temporary residents on that side of town, or maybe because we did not have the information to actually enroll in school, but we left the house Monday through Friday to go to the Y.

I made a friend, Miracle, who had to be about the same age as me. She was the only one who was even close to my age anyways. I quickly found out that she had problems. If I ever thought I was a bad liar, Miracle took the cake—and ate it, then said someone else did.

Our friendship was rocky, I remember my first day going to the Y, and Miracle, who had been there for some time was assigned to the group that I wanted to be in. Not because the group was anything special, but because the group leader was the most handsome male specimen I had ever laid eyes on. I remember his name too, Corey. He was so much older than I was, but given my past, age honestly meant little. By that point, I was practically conditioned to believe that most older boys wanted to get into my panties.

Corey was tall and blonde with the most dazzling blue eyes. Where I grew up, we didn't really see many white people. Not the ones like him anyways. Refined and upright. The ones we saw were ran-down and missing teeth. They would walk the streets just like the black people that were addicted to the same drugs.

The crackheads.

I'm going to save my tangent about crackheads for another timeline.

Anyways, I was talking about life in the shelter and the group leader.

Yes, Corey was handsome. Plus, they paid him to be nice to us so I think I may have misread him a couple of times. So, when I was assigned to someone else's group, I had a meltdown. I didn't even give my group leader a chance. A lot of new things were all happening in rapid succession, and not being the group with the cute leader, combined with the feelings of being in a strange new place away from everyone that I knew was enough to send me over the edge. My brother and sister were in the program for younger kids, so I rarely saw them at all.

When the group leaders saw me wailing like my world was falling apart, they asked me what I would like to do. I told them I wanted to be in the same group as Miracle. Easily enough, they switched my group and I got what I wanted. I was happy with being able to stare in awe of him and having a reason to follow him around.

His face is so fuzzy now; all I see are blurs where his features should be. However, the feelings are still fresh.

I look back on our time in the shelter with fondness, honestly. They made sure we were never bored, on weekends they would take us out either to the movies or to the skating rink. I had many first times there too, and I'm sure it made me well-rounded. The first time I had ever been to a skating rink was when I went with that group. They made it possible for me to get on a canoe and go camping for the first time in my life. They did enforce bedtimes for kids though, which was nothing new, but the older kids got to stay up longer and I was always jealous because I missed the age cut off by six months.

I wish I could remember the name of that shelter because I would like to donate to them, or do something to give back, because they were really a place of refuge for my family.

I really hated to leave.

The first time I ever saw my mom actually take up for me was when Miracle told her mom I punched her in the stomach.

Now, I know I said that I was a little bit of a bully, but Miracle was supposed to be my friend, and I would not just randomly punch the girl in her abdomen for no reason.

I had punched her in the stomach though.

That is why I said she had problems. I'm upgrading that to *crazy*.

She TOLD me to do it.

I was not going to at first, but she was putting all kinds of pressure on me to do it.

So, I did.

Then, she went off and told her mom that I punched her in the gut, with a face full of fake tears.

My mother saw right through her act.

I remember watching the two moms go at it on the stairs, until the women that ran the shelter came and broke it up. I think I felt a sense of pride in that moment. Like, I actually had a mother that would come to my aide.

Even after that showdown, I did not want to leave.

Miracle thought that we could resume being friends after that, but I refused to be a pawn in her little sick games to get her mother's attention. I still have moments when I wonder how she turned out.

Screaming

I'm going to call my first stepfather The Oppressor, because while I want to preserve his identity, I also want it to be known that I still feel sourly about his existence. It's a lot better than just calling him Satan. I don't think anyone is more satanic than Satan, so I guess it's unfair to give away that title so freely.

I'm not sure how old I was at that time, but, The Oppressor had decided that he didn't want my sister and I hanging around his house anymore, stinking up his air with our foreign-child odor, and only my brother—who was his biological child—could stay. If my mother didn't agree to those terms, she was welcomed to leave with us.

She had a big choice to make.

Of course, she chose to rally is all together and move out of his house, because she loved her children, and either he accepted all of us, or none of us.

I'm kidding.

She dropped my sister and me off at my great-grandmother's house like a bag of trash, then peeled off down the street leaving behind only the screech of rubber on concrete.

Eventually, she came back and received us. It was a day I had least expected too.

I was outside playing with my friend three houses down when I saw her car pull up at the end of the driveway. Once my sister noticed, she joyously ran out to the car and hopped in. I, on the other hand, did not want to see her, let alone get in the car with her.

My life was finally normal.

I did not have to hide under beds, or be so concerned about making too much noise because a swift backhand would connect with my bottom lip.

I slept on a mattress that wasn't flushed directly with the floor, and probably one of the most important things, I felt loved in every way.

So, I did what any sane person would do and took off running towards my great-grandmother's house, yelling the whole way there. I just knew that if I yelled loud enough, she would hear me and rush out to save me.

I ran as fast as my little stubby legs would carry me. Screaming my heart out.

Suddenly, I had the wind knocked out of me as I was tackled to the ground.

I had not noticed my cousin in the car with them before, and it was she who jumped out of the backseat and slammed me against the ground, locking her arms around me to refrain my kicking.

When I looked up, there she was. So close, yet so far away. She had heard me screaming and ran out to save me.

Only it was too late.

They had me in the car and I remember the rev of the engine as the car howled off down the road.

I guess I can say I was kidnapped.

Every day after that I was full of hatred. The love and admiration that I harbored for my mother was replaced with bitterness and anger. My thoughts shifted from trying to please her, to masterminding several attempts to lock her away.

I disliked her for such a long time, and that moment was the trigger. I saw then that she did not care about anyone else's happiness but her own. I was just collateral damage in the dangerous games she played.

I'm sure by now you are thinking: "I thought you said your story isn't all bad?" and you're right. My story isn't all bad. I had good days growing up too.

There was a period of blindness in my life. Not physically, but like, a mental blindness. I didn't learn how to read until I was well into the second grade, so, I couldn't understand anything. Everything just looked like calligraphy. It made preparing for a report card response nearly impossible. So, I threw them all away. Every one of them. Even the ones that were resent never made it into the house. I just knew in my spirit that it was a bad report and I was going to be punished for it.

One day, I'd forgotten to throw my most recent one out of the window on the bus. It stayed in my backpack all the way home, and my mother was good at checking my backpack for homework. On this day, she was going through it and pulled out the report card and looked over it.

My stomach dropped.

To my surprise, the report was a good one and my mother treated us to a pizza party. That was a good day. It's also one of the fonder memories I have as a kid.

One thing that my mother always made certain was that we never had any idea we were impoverished. Sure, we couldn't have everything we wanted, but she always made sure we had everything we needed. We never went hungry, and although the clothes may have been from a thrift store, they were clothes nonetheless.

For that much, I must thank her.

She did try.

Sometimes I sit and wonder how things would have been had they gotten any worse. If she had never found the strength to leave The Oppressor, would my life be different? Would I have eventually been beaten to death? Or become so withdrawn I needed to be under 24-hour psychiatric care?

I feel the chuckle coming.

Even after all of that, I still ended up under the care of a psychiatrist. But not for problems relating to my childhood. No. The things that led me to a psychotic break happened during my teenage years and well into adulthood. I guess I never got adjusted.

Genuinely Amused

Some could argue that falling in love with a narcissist was destined to happen. That through my years of abuse and neglect it was fate that led me into the arms of a man who cares more about himself than anyone else on the planet.

Well, I don't believe in fate.

I do, however, believe that my attraction, and ultimately the plunge down the rabbit hole was largely because I'd developed an odd sense of arrogance myself.

But this part of the story isn't about him.

This story is about discovering how I ended up this way. How I found the power to conquer the demons that have haunted me for such a long time.

As I revisit these memories, it's like blowing the dust off an old trinket you find lying around the attic. My life is so full of those trinkets. A collection of them, if you will. But, I think that's all of us. We've all tucked little moments away, storing them with the hopes of never having to see them again. At least not until you need them.

I may have lived most of my life as something put away on a shelf. Something pretty to look at, but serves no real purpose. Like those porcelain dolls that stare off into eternity. Always silent. Always watching.

For years, I was told what a beautiful girl I am. So pretty, so smart, so well-mannered. I didn't understand. I hated to look at myself in the mirror and I completely avoided it as best I could. In my rationale, there was no logical reason that anyone should be handing out such false compliments, because in my eyes, I was hideous. I was a girl who could never do anything right. A girl who became so accustomed to crying herself to sleep at night that she didn't see the many good days for what they were.

There's a picture of myself taken when I was around six or seven here on the wall in front of my computer. Even though the picture doesn't trigger the memory of that day, I can look at it and say that I was a pretty girl. A little round in the face, but pretty. I had perfected the half-smile by that time. The smile that was more of a ward than an expression.

This also must be around the time I started to discover the physical things about myself. Even though I spent a little over a year trying to avoid being raped by Anthony, I didn't exactly know what is was he wanted. My sense of right and wrong was in full effect though, so I knew that I could never give it to him. No matter how sweet he pretended to be. It wasn't then. No. It was after we left there and went to live with my great grandmother.

First, there are few people I love more in this life than my great grandmother. She has been my unfailing strength. The only one who never let me go. So, during the time that we spent staying with her, I was probably the happiest I'd ever been as a kid. We lived with her off and on, so, the time we spent there naturally became the saving grace of that little girl.

What I discovered while living with her was that I had a little bump in my vagina, and if I pressed it, it felt good. *Really good*. But I couldn't convey exactly how it felt to anyone. I remember calling my mother into the bathroom upon my discovery, and letting her see this mysterious bump that just came out of nowhere. She assured me that I was not dying, and that it was perfectly healthy for it to be there.

She laughed at me.

But not in a maniacal, or shaming way.

She was genuinely amused.

Looking back at that moment now, I'm not sure how I would respond to my daughter who just found out about her clitoris either. Especially if she thought it was a bump she could die from. I may laugh too. One thing my mother didn't do was make me feel bad about it.

She left the bathroom.

But I didn't.

I just stayed in there poking at it for a while, wondering where it came from, and what was the tingling sensation that swept over me.

Using My Fingers

It wasn't long after that discovery that I had my first self-induced orgasm. It was like fireworks had gone off in my brain; my pupils may have dilated and everything. What built up to the moment that I would eventually connect with effective coping, was my obsession with Jason David Frank. I was so in love with him. Of course, I know him as Jason David Frank now, but back then to that little girl, he was just Tommy.

The White Ranger.

One of the coolest things about living with my great grandmother was the fact that she had cable. See, The Oppressor barely kept a TV in the house, let alone have cable on one. I could sit and watch television all day on the weekends, and until my grandmother would get home from work, during the week.

I was largely interested in the Power Rangers, and other shows with real people. People who were out there living life. I hadn't made the connection yet that these people were just acting out a script, and if you had told me that, I wouldn't have believed you anyways. They were people, just like me, that somehow ended up with better lives.

The first time I masturbated, it was by rubbing a comb on my bump. I had gone to the back room, and covered my head with a blanket—because everyone knows that when you're under a blanket, no one can see you—and just started pressing it. Moving it around in a circle. The more I did It, the better it felt. I remember saying, "Oh, Tommy..." until that final moment came. When the sparks flew.

Who knows where anyone else was. I was unaware what had just taken place, but in that moment, I felt a strange sense of relief. So, I got up and washed the comb off, then, went back to sitting in the living room as if nothing happened. That moment has stayed with me for a long time for one simple reason—it made me feel better. Masturbating made me feel better. The fantasy that I could be with Tommy, even if it was only in my mind, brought me such great comfort that I did it repeatedly.

No, not with the comb.

I discovered that I could get the same results just using my fingers.

That moment defined how I would view coping for years. No one would teach me a way, so I made my own. I became a habitual masturbator at seven-years-old. Although I didn't see it as a problem, I did my best to hide it. I would only do it when everyone was sleeping in the middle of the night.

It may not have started off as a problem, but eventually it turned into one. I had to masturbate several times a day and what once was done in the middle of the night, became something I did secretly while other people were in the room. That was only because there was the thrill of being caught.

I couldn't resist.

It felt too good.

It may have opened me up to being fondled more openly as well. I'll go more into it later, but for now, just put it in the back of your mind that I was molested a lot.

Voluntarily and involuntarily.

I'll go over voluntary now.

Perhaps it's easier to say that as a child, you don't really know what you're doing or what you're saying, and whether a child "comes on" to you or not, it's always wrong.

Always.

So, I guess there's really no such thing as voluntary molestation. But, in a way, I can say that I invited it a good two times.

The first time, my cousin, who was a teenager, was having casual conversation with me. I'm not sure how I got on the subject of private parts, but it just naturally seemed to gravitate that way.

Oh no.

Guys, I think I just realized how coached I was.

Something about the words and the way they came out. Because I couldn't have naturally gravitated my way into being molested. I didn't have that kind of skill at seven. Which makes me further realize how much of a predator my cousin was back then.

But, to keep the story going, he asked me a question about my bump (clitoris) and when I couldn't really describe it to him, he asked me to show him.

My Mama Clara was downstairs sleeping and I was afraid I would wake her up. He told me to just go in the bathroom, pretend to use it, and just take my panties off.

I listened to him.

When I came back, he asked me if I liked the way it felt when I touched it. I didn't lie. It did feel good when I touched it. It felt equally as good when he touched it.

He started with his finger first.

Then, he unzipped his pants and pulled out his penis.

I don't remember what I expected then. But he rubbed it on my bump a few times.

Maybe he started to feel bad, and guilt started eating away at him or something, because he just stopped. Got up and walked out of the room.

There's another one of those family secrets that went under the rug. From that day though, I held a candle for my cousin. In my little childish mind, I thought he loved me.

That cousin went to jail for at least a decade on charges unrelated. He was one of Harris Counties Most Wanted people at one point in time too.

Even after he returned home from prison, and I was much older, I still had this strange attraction to him. I'm not sure what you would call that.

But that attraction was only fueled by the fact that I wanted to have sex with him, and briefly, he wanted to have sex with me too. I wasn't a virgin anymore.

How screwed up is that?

Nonetheless, I talked to my immediate family about it, and I think my sister was the one who made me come to my senses. *I had completely lost my mind.* Something about trauma bonding; although it was hard for me to view what had happened as trauma.

I can just hear the backlash from the rest of my family right now. I probably should have just gotten over it, right?

They thought I told so many stories.

Well, I guess they will really hate me now.

I must say that when I look at him now, all I see is a broken man who lost a lot of time. When Mama Clara passed—she was like a mom to me, but she was actually his mom—we both went into a deep depression. Mine lasted for a little over a year, and I don't think he's gotten out of his yet.

I can't make any excuses for what he did, but I will say that he was remorseful, which is more than I care to say for anyone else.

In My Fantasies

Remember when I said I started to learn the art of manipulation? Yeah, I got extremely good at it. It was all a matter of who you could get to believe what, and for how long. As I got older, around eight or nine, it became much easier for me to turn people against each other. Make people take my side. I built positive relationships with my teachers from second grade onward, not because I genuinely cared for them, but because they all had something to give—and would give it freely if they felt obligated enough.

I preyed on that in people. Forcing them into feelings of obligation. You didn't want to help me because **I** *wanted you to help me*, you wanted to help me because **you** *wanted to help me*. I learned how to get away with so much at school and for every ten wrongs, only one would get reported.

It worked well at home too.

By the time I was nine, my mother had finally gotten over The Oppressor once and for all. There were no more sightings of him for years at a time. A new player joined the game—we'll call him Dad. When he started to come around, I never knew what a Dad was, or how to even treat one, so I called him by his first name. He isn't a bad guy. From nine to adulthood, he's never been a bad guy. A little standoffish, but a great guy nonetheless.

At first, he was just my mother's resident boyfriend, so it stands to reason that I didn't think he would be around long anyways. Just like many of the other men that came and went, I didn't think it would be important enough to get to know him, or anything else for that matter. The difference with him is, he brought along two girls. Both much younger than me. I didn't harbor any resentment for them, they were cute kids. I don't think I ever really viewed them as sisters though. Just two little girls that moved in and would be staying for a while before leaving. They were fun to play with and I liked that. Still, I suffered from my own inner turmoil.

There was nothing much that I could do beside try and pretend the first eight years of my life weren't tumultuous. I had to pretend that I didn't hate myself as much as I did. The only thing that I could do was fantasize about what my life could be like. I would sit up for days, and just imagine the great things that happened in other people's lives as if they were happening to me. In my fantasies, I was happy. Loved. Respected. No longer the invisible girl that everyone saw without seeing. I spent a decade trapped in that mindset. I guess it pays to reason that I would have been as successful at writing as I was.

I recall the fourth grade, when writing is a pretty big deal. Mrs. Schultz would get up there and teach her heart out about writing—the jargon, grammar, and spelling. I was so fascinated with it. All of it. That's when I started to do it all the time. I excelled at writing in elementary. Often being chosen to read the things that I wrote for the class. Maybe that's when I discovered that I have a knack for storytelling. The attention was certainly welcomed.

There was this one homework assignment that involved writing, but I didn't have the time to write it at home. I can't remember exactly what the prompt was, but I do remember being called on to read my paper to the class. I wasn't prepared at all. But I couldn't say I didn't do my homework—I was afraid. So, with the rest of the class sitting on the carpet in front of me, wide-eyed and patiently waiting, I gave them a story. I would flip the pages in the packet as if I were really reading from my homework. When I was finished, everyone clapped. My teacher smiled as she took her place back in front of us and told me that it was a very good, well-thought out story. Then, she asked to see me by her desk once sharing was over.

I knew I was in trouble.

As I stood next to her desk, I remember her looking at me with a warm smile, she said, "There wasn't anything on your paper, was there?"

I wanted so badly to lie. To try and explain myself. But she took my hesitation as the correct answer. I didn't get in trouble that day. She simply told me, "What you made up was really good, and I'm proud of you for trying. Now, your challenge is going to be writing the story you told."

3rd, 4th and 5th grade were great school years, and I'm sure it largely had to do with the district I had moved into. The teachers weren't mean and surly, and they had things that made us well-rounded individuals. The only thing about those years at that school was the fact that my teachers would go out of their way to spite my mother. When I was in the third grade, my mother was beginning her conversion to be a Jehovah's Witness, and naturally, we began to be raised that way.

If you don't know, as a Jehovah's Witness, you do not celebrate any of the national holidays, say a pledge of allegiance to the flags or any other nationalistic thing. I wasn't entirely against the change, I just knew it was different. I had to explain to my teachers why I wouldn't stand, why I had to be excused from the class during holiday parties, and they were simply intolerant of it. The principal of the school would call my mother in to talk to her about it, and my teachers would think they were doing me a favor by saving me bags of candy and cards. I was caught in the middle of it all.

It was the last day before winter break, during third grade, that I was sitting in line waiting for my bus when one of my teachers sat a bag with a bow on it next to me. She told me that the other teachers had gotten together to get me something for Christmas.

It was a nice gesture, but it didn't mean as much to me as they thought that it would.

No, my mother didn't take the present away and throw it in the trash. She let me keep it and after stating that they were only doing it to make a statement to her, she never mentioned it again.

By the time I was in the third grade, it didn't matter much that I wasn't supposed to celebrate Christmas, because honestly, I had NEVER celebrated Christmas a day in my life. Christmas was like one of those things that happened and then it was over. I think it was just the fact that we now had a religious basis for not recognizing Christmas as anything other than another day, that had people so upset about it. Because before that, it was just pure poverty and domestic abuse that didn't really get us all in the "giving" spirit.

Comfort

Forcing myself to revisit all the memories I've tried so hard to forget is tough. I soon realized after starting this project that there was a reason why I had suppressed these things for such a long time. Still, I'm finding myself more at peace these days. I'll often wake up from a dream that reminds me of one of those moments.

Last night it was just the sensation of running. The sound of my heart beating in my ears as it thuds rapidly inside of my chest. The rush of the wind as it whipped across my face. I've always been chubby—fat cheeks, round belly, and wide feet, but I ran quite often. Random races would pop up between my siblings and I at any place and any time. My brother was the fastest. Even though I always came in last, it never stopped me from trying to prove myself.

My brother would do this thing called "The Booster" where he would take my hand and run as fast as he could so that I could gain more speed. It was more of a confidence booster than anything else.

While we're on the topic of my younger brother. There are many things that I love about my brother, but there are other things that really used to get to me. We're almost three years apart, which isn't that much of an age gap, but it's enough for hIm to be labeled the annoying little brother.

We got into our fair share of fights right up until he started to get bigger and stronger than me. I did things to make him mad on purpose, not because I didn't like him, but just to see his reaction. He would do this thing when he got mad where he would puff his cheeks out really big and ball his fist at his side, the whole time breathing heavily through his nose and blowing snot everywhere.

It was funny.

But only because I knew he didn't want to fight me.

My sister and I took turns getting him in trouble too. Which is sad on our part, but, he made it easy. Whenever he would tell a lie, he looked down at the ground all sad-like. We used that against him, even when he wasn't lying but had just accepted that he was going to get a whooping.

I can recall one time when he embarrassed me so much. I may have gone on a campaign to get him in trouble as much as I could without anyone catching on.

See, there was this boy that lived in our apartments that was the cutest. He was a little older too, so that added even more to his appeal. Naturally, because I was the oldest of our group, I should have had first dibs.

It didn't work out that way, let's just say that.

The boy, Patrick, and my brother naturally made a connection just on the account that they were both outgoing boys, despite my brother being only about seven or eight.

It's funny to me now that I realize that my brother has always acted older than he actually is. Which may largely have to do with him being the only boy in a group of four girls.

Anyways, I don't remember what made me confess my attraction to Patrick with my brother. I may have just said it in passing. But the next thing I know, one night he blurted it out to Patrick.

He was young.

He still had to pay though.

Patrick rejected me as anything more than a friend, or a neighbor, and I may have very well slept under my bed that night.

Call it a comfort thing.

As I think about it now, I would spend a lot of time under my bed. It was like a shelter from the rest of the world whenever I wanted to disappear.

I can honestly say that my relationship with my brother hasn't really changed much over the years. Of course, I've grown to have a greater appreciation of him as an adult, but from childhood onward, we've pretty much have always gotten along.

He is entitled though.

I blame my mother for that. She chose him as the favorite a long time ago and that was something I accepted within myself, since I knew that I would never be good enough for anyone.

My brother was the Prince—he added the Charming later in life.

When we were growing up, my mother catered to him for one reason: he was the boy she wanted, with the man she wanted.

Couldn't beat that.

If you ask her now, she will probably deny it. Say she loved us all equally.

Tell her she's lying, for me, will you?

Nonetheless, I don't blame my brother for any of the things that happened to us while we lived with his father, or for being able to stay when my sister and I were kicked out.

Now he thinks that he's supposed to get anything he wants, and to an extent he's still spoiled.

But my brother has come through for me more times than I can count. He's taken up for me, gotten things done, and is honestly only a phone call away for anything.

When I was younger, I would always say that it would have been better if it were only my sister and I—we didn't need a brother. That's so far from the truth. Having a brother like mine is a blessing.

I don't think I tell him I love him enough.

Separated

Being attractive is a gift. Being attractive and not knowing it? Well, that's a bag of cats.

By now you should know that I was called a pretty girl for most of my childhood. I heard it so often that it became one of those things that you just expect people to say. None of those words meant anything to me.

They were just that—words.

My run-in with Anthony wasn't the last time something like that happened to me. This time, it was a little closer to home.

The guy was practically family.

Around the time that I was in the third grade, we lived in an apartment complex that was right around the corner from my great grandmother's house, so naturally, I spent a lot of time over there. My cousin had a paternal cousin that would come around her house often. In my mind, if the guy was the cousin of my cousin, he was my cousin too—if that makes any sense. Anyways, he wasn't a bad guy either, always so nice.

That's how they get you.

One day I was walking with my brother and sister from school when we saw my cousin out walking. My siblings ran off to meet him in the distance and left me struggling to catch up. It's unclear to me how we had gotten separated. That part is a little hazy. But I remember what happened next with clarity.

I lost them.

For a moment, I was wandering around before deciding to go back home, figuring that's where they would go anyways. As I was cutting through the neighborhood, the cousin of my cousin saw me—we're going to call him Scum—and told me that I looked thirsty.

It was hot outside.

I didn't see a problem with following him into his house for a glass of water.

The house was filthy.

Mounds of clothes everywhere.

Trash.

It smelled like old, sweaty gym socks.

I remember lingering by the door for a while, then he told me I could sit down and get comfortable while he went into the kitchen. When he came out with the glass in his hand, I was sitting on the couch, looking around but not saying a word.

He sat so close to me that he was almost on my lap.

After taking several sips of the water, I noticed that it didn't taste right. Something was off about it. I sat it down and scooted away from him, feeling the tension in the room get thicker as he just sat there with his eyes locked on me.

I was uncomfortable, and I'm not sure what made me stick around as long as I did. When I moved away, he moved closer, putting his arm around my shoulder this time.

I stiffened.

Next, he reached his other hand up and hooked the collar of my shirt with his index finger and pulled at it so that he could look at my budding breasts. I jumped up from the couch and ran out of the door. I didn't stop running until I was practically home.

The saddest part of this story probably isn't the fact that it happened, but the things that happened afterward.

See, I told my family what happened and I may have done it in such an indirect way, they all thought I was joking.

No one believed me.

He told them it was all in my head and that I had made the whole thing up. Therefore, my family dismissed the whole notion of it. Scum still came around, was invited to all the family functions. But he never touched me again, and I was never left alone with him.

I guess that was a good thing.

I may have been inclined to believe that it was all some wild story that I made up in my head if years later he didn't proposition me for sex.

Consensual sex.

The man genuinely wanted me to consent to have sex with him. The fact that he still wanted to see me naked is the scary part.

When I was twenty, one of my cousins had an engagement party, which I attended, and got so drunk I was blacking out. I didn't have my own vehicle at that point in my life, so I was making due with bumming rides. I don't exactly remember how I ended up in the car with Scum and his girlfriend, but I was sitting in the backseat behind her, while he drove. I didn't really think much of it at first, until I realized through my drunken stupor that he was rubbing my thighs.

It's as if after all those years, he was just lying in wait. Didn't work out so well when I was eight, so maybe I would see reason at twenty?

The sight of that man disgusts me.

He still comes around.

He will still send me random messages online that start with, "Hey beautiful."

I came straight out and asked him, "You still want to get in my pants, huh?"

You know what he said?

"I want to treat your body gentle, and suck on you until you cum…"

That's what he told me.

What do you call a person like that?

What kind of person does it make me?

I look at his daughter now. She's starting to get up to the same age I was when he tried looking at me.

She's a round thing too.

Part of me wants to talk to him about what he did. What the mere sight of him continues to do; but he already looks so broken. The last time I saw him he just looked so tired and sad.

They say there's no rest for the wicked.

I think part of me wants to rationalize the whole thing, for the sake of his daughter. I want so badly to believe that it was all just in my head—a story I made up. The lie would just be so heavy, and the whole goal is to throw off these weights, right?

What happened to me was no dream. It was no part of my imagination. I must accept that. For all these years, I've just buried this.

I've buried all of this.

Now that it's coming out into the open, I feel the cleansing happening. Like a soothing balm spread across my skin.

I like it.

I Had Given Up

I'm blessed to say that I was never raped as a child—not sure how I would have handled that back then. Up to my teen years, I only had close calls.

But, while I may not have been raped, I was molested in other ways. I can't figure out why these things happened to me, all I know is that everyone got away with it.

At least in the justice system, because not a single one of them was ever brought up on charges.

It was just swept under the rug, and I essentially had to pretend as if they are all just wild stories. It only made my case worse when I started writing stories of my own.

There I was thinking I was making everyone proud of my writing, when really, they were just using it to make me seem like I was trapped in a world of make-believe.

The last time anyone had inappropriate contact with me, was about the same time as Scum. They were all friends. Maybe he told them that I was ok with it.

The eight-year-old that no one would believe even if they did have a little touch or two.

This guy was deaf.

The age of the video game was still fresh, and my cousin had a PlayStation. His friends would come over and spend the night, and we would all take turns playing the game.

One night the deaf guy—henceforth, Chester—was staying over at my great grandmother's house on a weekend I had chosen to stay, and just like any other time, we were all in my cousin's room playing the game. As it got later, everyone just started to fall asleep.

Except Chester.

No. Chester stayed up burning the midnight oil on his game.

For a while he and I were taking turns, until I had fallen asleep. I remember feeling strange.

You know when you're in that part of sleep where you're not fully asleep, but not quite awake either?

Well, the discomfort woke me up.

I'm not sure how long he had been down there with his fingers in my vagina, but when I woke up, that's where they were. As if he had misplaced something, and needed to look in my panties to find it.

Because Chester was deaf and I was a conjurer of stories, no one took me serious when I told them. So, just like everything else that had been going on, I just tucked it away too.

I think Chester may have died a few years ago. I'm not going to say that his death would have been Karma. I will say that I probably wasn't the first, or last, little girl he touched inappropriately.

After a while, I believe I just accepted the fact that I would be fondled.

Older guys would want to touch me.

Put their nasty lips on me.

See me naked.

There wasn't a single thing I could do about it, and so I had given up.

I'm going to move up on the timeline a little bit and take you to the time I *was* raped—while we're on the topic.

As I mentioned, it didn't happen when I was a child, instead, I was nineteen. I had the whole free-spirit thing going on, and I think that was the part that blinded me to what was happening.

It's funny that when I tell this story to people—because unlike some of these other stories, this one is public knowledge—I make it seem like I wasn't affected at all by it.

Just the other day, I think I laughed about it with a group of friends.

Now, during these free-spirit years, I was sexually active with just about anyone that said hello and lingered around too long, it's not something I'm proud of, but hey, it happened.

There was this security guard that worked for the college, making sure no one gained access without an ID badge. It was never really my intention to show him anything other than an ID, but I think I may have flirted with him one too many times.

Perhaps that's why he thought it was okay.

Of course, I was a big flirt, so I didn't think anything of it. Fast forward a couple of months, and the guy was fired. It wasn't long afterwards that I received a phone call in the middle of the day asking me what I was up to and if I had time to talk. It was the security guard, Gary Washington, who had gotten my number from Lord knows where. He continued to explain to me the reason he was fired and that now he could talk to me *seriously* since he didn't have a conflict of interest anymore.

It didn't dawn on me that I had never given the man my number and that him calling me completely out of the blue was just plain creepy. Nonetheless, I entertained him for a while. When he asked if we could meet up that night, I didn't object, figuring that it would be fine.

Well, it was not fine.

He came over to my parent's house, and we talked outside for a while before he suggested that we go get something to eat.

I'm going to blame myself here for being stupid and not speaking up when I felt the vibes shift, or when we passed up quick places to eat and got on the freeway, speeding across town. Now, I've never been the best at directions, but I'm sure driving twenty minutes to go to a Burger King is just bad.

So, there we were closer to his apartment and my nerves were trapped in my throat. *I did not want to have sex with him.*

He was unattractive, stood about 6'9 and was overweight.

370lbs overweight.

Plus, he had that smell that overweight guys have when they don't bathe properly—it made my stomach hurt.

But I was too nice.

I've always been too nice.

Equal parts gullible too, I guess.

He took me to his apartment where I could eat my burger first. Every bite contained more anxiety than the last. I should have asked to go home—I shouldn't have even allowed him to take me clear across town. That had to be the most painstaking burger I've ever eaten.

I remember him tugging at my shirt and telling him to stop. The sound of him tearing my t-shirt makes me shudder to this day.

The sound of him tearing my t-shirt makes me shudder to this day.

Call me what you want, but this is where I decided to just give him what he wanted. He overpowered me, yes, but that's what rape is, isn't it? An act of power.

So, I just gave it up.

If I were going to be raped, I didn't want any bruises or scars to come along with that. Still, he tore me.

Ripped me.

Bound my hands together as he rammed into me like a MAC truck.

So many things were racing through my mind. I wanted to scream.

Cry. Run.

But I had no idea where I was, and I didn't have a cellphone since I'd stupidly left it in the house. The only way to get back home was to just lay there. Holding it all in.

When he rolled over, it wasn't long before he was sound asleep. That could have been my moment to just sprint for the door.

But I was afraid. Trapped.

A cage without bars.

I think he knew that. He knew that I wouldn't go anywhere—and I didn't.

I looked over at the clock after fifteen agonizing minutes went by and then I nudged him. "My parents are going to be looking for me. I should go now." My voice was so shaky.

He hopped back up, forced me back into position and did it all over again.

I was so sore as I walked back to his truck that night. Unsure what would happen next. Would he really take me home, or was he taking me to the woods to drop me off in a pre-dug hole? He threw the truck keys at me and told me to take myself home while he slept on the passenger side. I didn't say much aside from asking for directions to get myself home. Once we got to an area that I recognized, I could navigate the rest of the way without him.

When I saw my house, I wanted to run inside and hide under the covers.

Just shut myself away from the world.

Once I slammed the door to his truck, he told me: "Don't be a stranger."

As calmly as I could, I went inside and got into the tub. Intent on pretending it never happened.

I had grown accustomed to forcing things away, and it just made sense to do so. It was a few months later that I came out and told my grandmother about it, and she was able to effectively walk me through what happened and helped that part of me to heal again.

A Little Ironic

I've always been quite vocal about being suicidal.

This way, no one can genuinely say they never knew.

I've felt alone for most of my life. It's one of those crushing feelings that never really went away, even though people huddle around me.

Deep down, I know they will never understand. My life really doesn't matter, but if I leave, that means they must do things for themselves.

They won't sincerely miss me. Just the idea of me. The idea that they'll always have someone there when they find themselves in a rut. Someone that can help them out. Someone who they can project their thoughts and insecurities on.

I guess that fine.

It's the thought of going through with taking my life that makes me sad, and the longer I think about it, the worse it gets. I came to view suicide as a healthy past time.

For years, I've been at complete peace with dying.

If that makes any sense.

I had the worst of it when I was a teenager. Things were just not taking off for me as I had hoped.

Life was happening for everyone.

Everyone except me.

At fourteen, the concept of suicide became real to me. I would sit and think of so many ways to end it all. Convinced that this wasn't the way my life was supposed to be.

The media contributed a large portion of that, I think.

Every channel, every magazine, every internet article—they all catered to the idea that being *thin was in*. When you're thin, people love you. They want to be around you. The Disney Channel was probably my biggest source of soul-crushing self-hatred.

Why did everyone have happy lives?

Why did it *always* work out in the end?

What's strange is that I kept watching, even when I would literally cry myself to sleep because of the emptiness I felt after binging their content.

One year around December I think I'd had enough of living. I had found acceptance in the fact that the world no longer needed me in it.

Maybe it was because she suffered from her own demons that my mother picked up on the warning signs. She wanted to take me somewhere to be evaluated. I liked that she was upfront about taking me to a psychiatric care unit, and so I didn't freak out when we arrived.

West Oaks was a nice, private facility, I guess. We only waited a mere 5 or 6 hours to be seen by their qualified mental health professional.

I'm being entirely sarcastic.

I was deemed worthy enough to be checked into the inpatient adolescent program in the middle of the night. They made me strip myself of a bra—because of the wires—and take the laces out of my shoes. I'm not sure if my mother anticipated me staying there—she may have just wanted me to talk to a psychiatrist—because she didn't bring any extra clothes. So, I checked into the unit with nothing but the clothes on my back.

My mother could walk to the back with me and help me get adjusted. I knew my stay would be interesting when upon my arrival, a girl with butchered hair climbed over the circular desk to use the phone.

The men in all-white scrubs are real. That's not an urban legend they made up just for television.

They came and sedated her so quickly.

Everyone else in the program was asleep, so after showing me my room and bidding me to hug my mother goodbye, I was promptly asked to go to bed.

I was locked away for about a week—and if it wasn't a week, it felt like one.

My roommate was homicidal—which seemed to be a little ironic.

I wanted to kill myself and she wanted to kill other people. I guess we were tailor-made for each other. We weren't friends though. She barely talked at all. Which probably should have scared me more than it did.

The one friend I made was this large, black girl that was a few years older than me. She seemed to be quite sane compared to the other people that were stashed away in there. Including, but not limited to, the girl that walked around interacting with at least ten people. Her name may have very well been Allison, but honestly, she called herself a lot of things. I remember watching her sit there all day and talk to herself. Sometimes, she would slap her face and glare off into thin air with a look of pure surprise.

I spent Christmas under psychiatric evaluation.

My family didn't just lock me up there and throw away the key though, they took the time to come and visit me. I remember the conversation that I had with my aunt one day. She told me that I had to get better—that I didn't belong in a place like that. She believed nothing was wrong with me.

Even things said with a mild tongue can sting. I believe that she really had the best of intentions.

I do.

The thing I couldn't quite understand, and even now to this day, is how people can be so quick to tell someone to just get over it. Just get over your illness and act like it never happened. I blame that, in part, on the overall black community.

As black people, we are so engrained to dismiss mental illness as just a "lack of faith," that it's easy to say things that we think are encouraging, but are, in fact, having the opposite effect.

But teen me didn't see any of that. I took her at her word and put on a grand show to convince my psychiatrist and the other nurses in the unit that I was close to cured. Just so they could let me out.

Nothing was wrong with me.

But why was I still dying inside?

Why didn't I feel any better?

I left West Oaks in the same shape I was in when I entered. Only now, I had to continue the show because everyone thought I was fine. Better than fine. Cured of my suicidal demons.

I wanted so bad for it to be true. I thought for a long time that if I pretended it was, then it would eventually happen. I would be okay.

That was my last stay in a program like that. It became one big joke with my other family, and something that my mother would use to threaten me with if I didn't behave.

I locked myself deeper into my fantasies. They were my only escape. All I would want to do is lay awake in my bed and think about all the fabulous things that could be happening for me—one day. To be left alone to my thoughts was all I asked for, and for the most part, I went unbothered.

Then, it kind of started to get out of control. I wasn't bathing, barely eating, when I was at school, I couldn't focus on anything. Just the images in my head. The perfect world that I had built for myself.

My grades started to suffer. I wasn't writing anymore. I was essentially just a vegetable.

Catatonic.

The walking dead.

In ninth grade, I started to see my school counselor for a couple of reasons: I wanted to get out of class, and I wanted help. I was still on a mission to see my mother either locked away, or being taken from her so that we could start a new life. So, in that regard, I would show that counselor bruises from a whooping I rightly deserved and counted on her to report it to CPS.

CPS never did anything. They would come out and harass my mother though, and make it seem as if they were going to do an investigation, but we only ever saw them for the initial visit and suddenly they would close the case. Even when my mother was so bold as to pack bags for us and have us wait for the case workers to take us away—but they never did.

Their failure to act threw my plans off every time, and eventually I was forced to try and find new ways to start a new life.

Anyways, I came to view my counselor as my friend, which means that she was doing her job, and she would help me work out some stuff that was going on with me. The only guidance that she gave was letting me draw my own conclusions. She was just there to listen to my stories. But she never heard these. Not the ones in this book. She knew how lonely I felt though. She knew my feelings of worthlessness.

I think she may have took it upon herself one day to try and orchestrate a meeting between a boy and I. Apparently, he had been talking to his counselor about me, expressing his feelings, and his counselor talked to mine. They both agreed that hooking us up would be good for us.

Only I didn't see it that way. I took it as a complete betrayal of my trust, and I didn't go back to see her anymore after that. Granted, I knew the boy. He was one of the funniest guys I knew at the time and he made me laugh and feel good about myself. I'd known he had a crush on me for a long time, but I never knew that it was deep enough for him to talk to his guidance counselor about it.

That boy is dead now.

It still makes me sad when I think about it too. Not only because he passed away, but because before the accident that took his life, he'd messaged me. He just wanted to hang out again, like we'd done several times as adults. That message hasn't been deleted, even though it makes me tear up. I know he'll never be able to respond. I bought a Coke bottle with his name on it just that I could share one last drink with him.

A Foolish Girl

By the time I was fourteen, my mother had dedicated her life to being a Jehovah's Witness and was strict about everything. Even before her baptism, she was like a drill sergeant. She closely monitored every-single-thing we did, and it wasn't much that escaped her attention.

There was this girl, Lotus, in the congregation that I just didn't like. Not for any reason of her own either, because she was a sweet girl. But she was everything I wanted to be.

Skinny.

Lighter-skinned.

Long, straight hair.

I hated her.

I'm quite sure my feelings toward her was closely aligned with one of the deadly sins. It ran so deep.

My disgust was fueled by pure envy, because I hated myself. Maybe she never caught on to the fact that I truly didn't like her, because she always smiled and waved. When my sister began her study of the bible, guess who came over and taught her?

I became obsessed with showing everyone that I wasn't the rotund, loser that I felt they all thought I was. So, I would do little things that I look back on now and just shake my head.

Such a foolish girl.

We spent a few years in that congregation, and my repulsion of her never wavered. When I was around 16, I really took an interest in this one guy—well, two guys.

The first guy was like a trophy, and the second guy was like a second-place ribbon.

Barry and Mason.

Those are obviously not their real names. But their actual names do rhyme. I only changed the first letter, in fact.

Anyways, I was hot for Barry. I just knew I would marry him and ride off into happily ever after with him. He was a tall, dark-skinned guy, that only had about three rotating suits; his favorite of the three was the purple one.

That darn purple suit. I told myself that after I married him, we would sit down and cut it up together.

He was a friend, but he was also standoffish, so that made it a little harder to get my foot in the dating door.

When I think back now, I was also much younger than him, so I'm not surprised he acted the way that he did.

Still, in my little pubescent eyes, our future was set in stone; that is, until my family took a trip to Huntsville with Mason and his mom. Then, everything changed. I jumped the Barry ship.

Mason may not have been as handsome, but he was funny. The guy was going places. Fluent in Spanish, valedictorian, great grammar and well-spoken. I never paid any attention to him until that trip.

What may have latched me to him, was that I perceived that he kind of liked me too. He didn't come right out and say it, but there was something there, and I wasn't ready to let go yet.

I needed to make sure that Lotus didn't steal him away. So, my cousin and I stayed up one night making prank calls. I let her do all the talking. It may have been around midnight one weekend and her number was the last one of the night. I told my cousin to say that Lotus should stay away from Mason because we had "homies in the hood" that would beat her up if she went near him.

It was such a childish thing.

Perhaps if she had gotten to speak with her on the phone, it wouldn't have been so bad, but I had my cousin leave that message on the voicemail.

It didn't take long for it to get back to me. I thought I had all my bases covered. It wasn't my voice on the message, after all. But alas, I was revealed as the culprit.

I tried to cover that up with so many lies. The more lies I piled on only made my punishment worse.

Being in high school didn't put me above corporal punishment, that's for sure.

Although I'm sure that Lotus knew I was involved, she never came out and said anything about it.

Honestly, she treated it as if it never happened—but the uneasiness was always present.

Mason and his mom moved away from the congregation. I think I held a candle for him—always thinking that someday we would be reunited.

The good news is that we were.

Nearly a decade later.

I wanted there to be a spark there so badly when we reconnected. The kind of spark that they have in the movies when two people go their separate ways and then reunite to discover that they've loved each other all along.

Our reunion was nothing like that.

Either he was just super nervous or he had a little intimidation going on, but he was awkward. I thought that maybe I could instigate something, just to kick things off on the right foot, but sadly, he turned me down flat.

Which was not something that I was used to.

Nonetheless, my flame fizzled out for him, almost as quickly as it appeared. I also quickly noticed that he parties a lot. Something that had stopped being my scene once I graduated college.

But that's neither here, nor there.

The Book Fair

I wasn't without my own flaws as a kid.

For a long time, I was consumed with proving that I had more than I did. Which I found hard to do in elementary—I mean, of course I could lie, but most of my lies never really added up.

The school book fair was a chance for me to prove that I was cool. A chance to make people like me.

There was only one problem: I didn't have any money.

Any money that my mother gave out was for jobs done around the house, and with five children scrambling for these little odd jobs to be done, was a joke. My brother almost always won. That may have been when I discovered how completely biased toward him she was. He was the son of The Oppressor, whom her love knew no bounds. Nonetheless, if I got anything it was only a couple of dollars at a time and I would take that straight to the Hispanic lady who sold nachos from her apartment.

Interesting side-note about the Nacho Lady—she took a fondness to me. She paid me $5 to help with her baby when she went out to run errands. That lady made me feel important. Even though I still had to pay for my nachos just like everyone else, she would always give me a little extra cheese.

Thank you, Nacho Lady.

Now, I was talking about the book fair. Alright, so one year when the fair came around my class went to preview what they had at first before we could come back the following day to shop. As I glanced around, I knew I had to have something—Sim City. My mother was big into playing The Sims too, so I thought it would be a nice gift for the both of us.

I tried to do things the right way, at first. I went home and asked my mother for the money to buy something, and she told me I would have to clean something.

I knew there had to be an easier way. I hated cleaning.

As if it had been written in the stars, I found this book of checks. I had learned how to fill out checks in class so I was semi-confident in my ability to make it look legitimate. Only I didn't have a clue about money itself. Sure, you buy things with it, but that was the extent of my knowledge.

I wrote that first check for $40. When I got to school, I was so excited, I couldn't wait to go to the fair and get the game. Unaware that the game was only about $20, I went to purchase the game, and do you know what that lady did?

She gave me change back!

My eyes were opened. I had just turned a check into cash. So, what was meant to just be a one-time thing, turned into a revolving door of check to cash. Soon, all my friends were noticing it too and wanted to get in on it.

I wrote everyone a check for $40, while I increased my payout to $50. I would tell them that they could go and buy whatever they wanted, if they brought me the change back.

I had so much money.

Even the kids in my apartment complex benefited, because after school, I would toss money down from the second floor. When my mother would ask where I was getting all the stuff from, I told her that one of my friends was giving me friendship gifts.

It went on for longer than I thought it would, to be honest. But when it all came tumbling down, I may have singlehandedly snowballed it. Probably more accurately described as an avalanche, really.

Everything happened in stages. First, she checked her bank account about a week later to find it missing a significant amount of money. Unaware where the charges came from, she contacted the bank and they sent her the printouts of the checks.

Didn't take a handwriting analyst to put together that it was written by a child.

She showed it to me first and asked me if I did. I'm sure she knew full well that it was me—but like the child I was, I denied it. Not only did I deny it though, I blamed my uncle's girlfriend, who is a known thief for giving me the checks and telling me how to fill them out.

She believed me, for the most part. His girlfriend was out of town and wouldn't be back for a while, so that bought me a little more time.

Keep in mind that cellphones were a luxury in those days, and they cost an arm and a leg for sixty seconds of talk time.

I remember the day my mother finally had a chance to talk to her though; we were at her boyfriend's house—who later became my stepfather—and I was playing with the kids in the back.

That conversation was so explosive, and when she called me into the living room, I knew my lie had finally unraveled and it was over.

So, I confessed.

At least I think I did. Wouldn't have mattered anyways, because within the next few minutes, my mother had left out of the apartment and came back through the door with a tree.

Yes, a tree.

It still had branches and leaves on it. Too large to be a switch.

The whole time she was breaking off the excess branches, there were sharp points on it now, and I was a babbling mess.

I don't know what kind of strange head games she was playing, but she asked me how many swats did I think I deserved, for not only stealing, but lying for weeks.

I went for the lowest number possible, hoping she would take mercy on me.

She doubled the number.

Of all my years of beatings, that may have been my worst one. I was bleeding by the end of it, that's for sure.

You would think that after ordeal, I would have learned my lesson. Well, let's just say that in middle school, I had the same little operation set up, only that time the account was closed—which made me logically conclude there was no way they could trace that back to me.

I got found out that time too.

She had to come to the school and pay the money back, and while she was at it, she took me out of school for the rest of the day and whooped me.

Now, that was the last time, and to this day, I don't even have checks to my own account.

All Over

Often things would begin to spiral out of control before they got any better. Even now I feel like I'm trapped in that loop sometimes.

I think at some point in life, we've all gone through a shoplifting phase. Some people are still trapped in that too. As adults. I'm not going to judge you if you are, but at some point, you should just grow up.

That's not me telling you how to live your life though.

I'm just saying.

My phase happened during my teenage years. I remember the first thing I stole: a purse, that I put random things in. Underwear, lipstick, and some candy. I did it not really for the things in the bag, but just to see if I could get away with it.

I walked right out of that store with my head held high, as if I was just an average shopper, all the while my heart was racing faster with each step.

Of course, since I got away with it that time, I started to shoplift pretty much everywhere I went. Except the mall, I never stole from a mall. Largely because I was never at the mall because of my short leash. So, mostly just from department stores and other operations. I wasn't by myself though, my brother and sister were in on it too. I would drive us to places just to shoplift and we would load up.

Our parents were never the wiser.

On our last go around, a family friend had come over to the house who was known for shoplifting. In fact, she had just had a run-in with loss prevention that sent her to the hospital and impounded her car. Maybe that should have tipped us off. But we were young, and didn't see harm in anything.

I was the driver for most of the day, but we rode around all day boosting clothes that we didn't need. She taught us how to test if the alarms in the front of the store worked, and how to play it off if it sounded.

But, I'm not going to give details on that.

Anyways, we hit up a few stores and it was at our last store of the night, my brother got out of the car and said something that we should have listened to. He said that he had a bad feeling about it.

Our confidence was soring. We had been getting away with stealing all day, why would we get caught now?

Well, we went into that store with our normal routine, not realizing the whole time that we were being watched. It wasn't until we were getting ready to leave that the man who had been following us approached and asked us to come quietly to the back.

My sister and brother took off running.

While the attention was on them, I headed in the other direction, gunning towards the bathroom as quietly as possible. I almost made it to.

Loss prevention grabbed my hands and pulled them forcefully behind my back before affixing the handcuffs.

Walking across the front of the store with my younger sister—who had gotten caught as well—in tow was like a walk of shame. I couldn't help but lower my head, not wanting anyone to see me.

That night I saw the door I never noticed before, and now every time I go into the store, I take a glance at it.

They sat us down in the small room and played back the camera footage. I couldn't look at it, so I just sat there trying to pretend to be tougher than the little girl I felt like on the inside.

They took all our information and I lied about my age, because at sixteen I could very likely have gone to jail. I told them I was thirteen and that I lived at a completely different address than my sister.

But once my sister had called our mother, it was all over. Besides that, my brother had gotten away and went home. She was up there within minutes and when she came in, she didn't speak a word, just reached back and slapped my sister and I repeatedly.

She had no idea we were handcuffed.

Strange how things took a turn that night, because aside from being smacked around, we didn't face any other consequences—but my mother went to jail that night.

Honestly, she'd talked herself right into the back of that squad car. All she had to do was keep it calm until we got home.

Her explosion and ultimate tantrum with the responding officer led her to say that he couldn't threaten her with jail because she had been before and could do it again.

Well, he called her bluff.

I remember going home that night and looking around the house, my mother had been busy being a mother—making dinner, cleaning—while we were out shoplifting. I felt bad.

When she called from the jail, I just had to tell her how sorry I was, because I didn't think we would ever get caught, nonetheless have her sent to jail for something we did.

I may have cried.

My grandmother was upset with us and took it upon herself to issue out our whooping, because my stepfather just didn't want to deal with anymore drama that night.

One thing about getting a whooping from my grandmother was that because she's older than most, she gets winded quite fast, so once she finished with one, we had to take an intermission so that she could regain her strength.

Alright, I'm going to go off on a little bit of a tangent right here, because I brought it up.

There is something about those days that I miss. If only being an adult was as simple as getting a whooping when you mess up and that was just about the end of your punishment. But could you imagine the kind of whooping you would get as an adult?

Don't pay your phone one month and an AT&T representative shows up with a belt. However, after your twenty lashes, your phone bill is current for the month.

I don't know.

That's the weird part of me coming out to say hello again.

A Little Baggy

In high school, I was only a couple of things: super cool, or insanely weird—but the good kind of weird.

None of those qualities warranted any of my male peers to take a second look at me though. I was always friended so quickly. The rejection may have very well just been in my head too. But for the most part, I liked high school. I didn't have those experiences of people bullying me or being strung up to the flag pole by my underwear.

People legitimately liked me.

At least I think they did.

Even if they didn't, no one ever came forward about it. I was cool with just about everyone who mattered—but that didn't make me popular. It made me relevant.

I really felt that my high school years were going to be my best ones yet…until I started getting sick.

Not the kind of sick that you can bounce back from either. I mean, passing out, I've fallen and I can't get up, kind of sick.

No one really noticed at first, I just looked odd. I had started to feel a little different too; lightheaded a little more often, confused, the feeling that my heart would leap out of my chest. But, I didn't take any of that for a sign that anything was seriously wrong with me. Something new started to happen though—boys at school started to take notice of me. Like real notice. Not just best friend notice.

There was this guy that played football, nobody really liked him because he never hit the showers with the other guys after practice, and so he was almost always musty. They had a name for him, but it would be rude of me to say it. However, he was handsome. Like, really-really handsome. We talked like friends for eighth grade and when ninth grade came around—little did I know so did the sickness—he started to address me as his "girl" which was strange for me.

I was equally embarrassed and flattered at the same time. Mix that right on in with teen angst and you have some self-destruction waiting to happen. However, he was just nice to me. Didn't want anything, didn't try to pressure me into anything, and I liked that about him. I think he was just unsure about himself too, since they would bully him. Maybe he thought that I didn't see him as the extremely handsome guy he is.

The world may never know.

He wasn't the only one though. There were others. It was the oddest thing! Boys would hold my hand, say little things to me to make me smile, leave me little notes.

I felt accepted.

But even more than that, something else was off.

My clothes were getting loose.

But not just like a little baggy, I mean like they looked like parachutes on me. I'm sure I could have landed safely on the ground if I were ever to leap from a building in those clothes. Unbeknownst to me, I was also losing weight.

Large amounts of it.

I went from roughly 320 pounds down to 197 pounds in a matter of months. So, it shouldn't have been much of a surprise to me that people started to take notice of me. When I look back on that time in my life, I must admit that I looked very much ill. There was definitely something wrong with me.

Nonetheless, I was happy for the attention. It only reassured me that these were going to be the best years of my life. Boys liked me, I had friends, I was just learning to drive.

Everything was finally coming together.

That's when all the negative side effects started to happen. The fainting spells, paralysis and migraines, on top of a slew of other things. I was stuck at home more often than I was at school, which became a problem for my mother.

By tenth grade, she'd had enough. She pulled me and my sister from school one day and told us that we would be home-schooled. I didn't think the idea was that bad at first. It meant that I no longer had to wake up early in the morning, at least.

However, that became the least of my worries. I went from waking up early in the morning for school, to waking up early in the morning for the nurse to draw blood or check my blood pressure.

That was the beginning of my week-long stays in the hospital. For most of my childhood, I had never really been a sickly kid, I don't recall having to go to the hospital at all, really. But when I was high school, all of that changed, almost overnight.

It was the first time any of us had heard of Graves' Disease, or Hyperthyroidism, and when the doctor told us that it's hereditary, everyone assumed it was from my father's side of the family.

That ended up not being the case. Years later, we found out that my grandmother's half-sister had the same thing, and she eventually had to have her thyroid completely removed.

I liked the "new and improved" version of myself too much to take my medicine. I just knew that the moment I started to take it, I would go back to being unaccepted and unloved.

I spent a lot of time in the hospital because of it.

We May Be Due

I should probably talk about my siblings a little more. About how our relationship grew over the years. We have some interesting memories.

As the older sister, I was the mastermind of most of our great adventures—which largely involved getting money.

Every now and again, I would tell my siblings that we were all going out to "help" mother with some of the bills around the house, so we should go from door-to-door and asking our neighbors for money. In fact, we should all dress up in our uniforms so that we could look "professional."

I had so many get-rich-quick schemes going on. But somehow, I always managed to get caught. I think that taught me to play the long-game, and not just look at the smaller picture.

My brother and sister were always so supportive of my dreams. Even as kids. We would take turns getting each other in trouble by agreeing to different ploys.

My two step-sisters eventually moved away to Miami with their mother and for the remainder of our teen years, we didn't see them. They weren't around when my sister got pregnant with my nephew.

Let's talk about the middle child for a moment.

My sister and I have generally always been best friends. Even when we hated each other. Which sounds strange, but it's true. I don't think there was ever a time when we went longer than a month without speaking to each other. Sure, we would have our arguments just like sisters are supposed to have, but we always make back up.

Speaking of, I think we may be due for a falling out soon.

Nonetheless, we've always been there for each other. Except she's never really known my inner battles, in their entirety, because I still see her as too young to understand.

We briefly had a conversation about it years later. She told me that she apologized. Not for her.

For them. For the family that didn't believe me. For me having to experience those events.

Even though I told her there was no need for apologies, it was all water under the bride, I must admit that it kind of felt good hearing it. Almost as good as it feels getting everything off my chest after all these years.

She's still waiting for the whole story. So many things she doesn't know about me. Stuff I wanted to guard her from.

Even now I think that I still see her as my little sister, and she's married with three children now. She'll always be the little girl that would snitch on everyone even though she was in on it too. I didn't really hold my sister in high-esteem when we were living with The Oppressor. She was just always willing to do what mother said. Not that I blamed her—she was still so young.

As I began my descent into teenage-introversion, my sister and I started working at McDonald's. We went in for the interview together and got the job together; things started to take off in her life while mine just seemed to be teetering from her success.

One thing I must say about her, is that she is a hard worker. She believes in putting her all into her work. And well, me, I just give the bare minimum. Especially when it's something that one, I don't want to do, or two, I feel like I'm too good to do.

I have my hang-ups.

Anyways, she met this guy that she fell in love with and the next thing everyone knew, she was sneaking off to be with him. Of course, I knew about some of their secret meet-ups, because my mom was still very much strict—but I never told.

It was when she had to go to the hospital one day that we all found out that she was pregnant.

My initial reaction was happiness. I was excited at the fact that I would be an aunt. Then, an awful seed of jealousy was planted in my heart.

I couldn't shake the feeling that it was supposed to be me. I was supposed to be the one to give my mother her first grandchild. I felt as though she was taking something from me. Afterall, I am the oldest, and there she was not only going off and losing her virginity before me, but then bringing home a baby before me too.

I was so green.

Emerald green.

Hulk green.

I quit my job at McDonald's because of unfair work conditions and continued my self-induced hatred for my sister, who kept working and bringing home money.

After I blew my last paycheck, I was just over having a sister that I felt was spending her life trying to make me look bad. As if I were good for nothing.

It's crazy seeing these words.

The thought of actually having such a disdain for my own sister just makes me feel bad. Because I know what kind of person she is, and she may be a lot of things, but I know that she never had any ill-intentions towards me.

Of course, that's what I realize now that I'm an adult. Back then, my thoughts were different.

For all purposes, my sister is going to be known as Rose. Because although she has her thorns, she has been such a symbol of love and boldness.

So, moving on, eighteen-year-old me didn't really like my sister. Plus, she was just a crappy pregnant person. That's no joke. I have no idea why being pregnant makes her so volatile.

For most of her pregnancy, I had made up in my mind that I wouldn't have anything to do with the baby. I would just make it stay out of my way since I would be forced to live with it for a while.

By this point both my sister and I were high school drop outs, and my parents had moved us across town. Rose wanted to go back to school and finish for the sake of her baby. Just to say she completed something, maybe.

I said that if she went back to school, I would go back to school because I couldn't have her going out and finishing high school while I sat at home and looked pitiful.

That's exactly what we both did. Only, about a semester into the accelerated program, I lost interest because I felt as though I was too grown to be back in high school. Eventually she stopped attending as well.

The closer it was time for the baby to arrive, the closer I started to feel the need to prove that I could make a baby too.

So, I went out and gave my virginity away to a stranger I had met on the internet.

It's so strange, really. Sitting here thinking about all the warning signs that I had blown right past.

Long hours on the computer.

Browsing online-dating websites.

Crazy amounts of time on Myspace.

The whole thing just seems surreal now, and the memories are a lot clearer.

I remember my first inappropriate internet run-in. Not being experienced wth the number of freaks there are out in the world, and just being plain gullible, I was thrilled when this guy wanted me to video chat with him. In the age of the webcam, my mother had gotten her first laptop that already had one installed—so, I switched from our desktop and to her laptop to video chat with the guy. Low-and-behold, the guy wanted me to watch him masturbate. I watched him blankly at first, with my camera turned off.

Watching guys masturbate does nothing for me—I'm sure that there are some women out there that are turned on by it, but, for me it was a waste of time, and I'm not sure why I even stayed connected.

I'm not sure why I did a lot of things that I did at that age.

Well, I had been hiding in my mother's room with the lights out, which I realize now wasn't the best place to hide, but I went unbothered for a long time. Until she came bursting into her room, and there I was staring at a penis being constantly stroked.

She wanted to be mad.

Wanted to hit me.

But, she didn't do either of those things. Instead, she told me that since I was eighteen, she was going to allow me to make my own decisions and mistakes, and she hoped that she had trained me well enough to make the right choices in life.

That may have been everything I needed to just go for it.

I wanted a baby too, and I was going to get one, even if it didn't have a father to go with it. I had to show that my baby would be cuter than hers, and I would be the better mother. I would raise my child to be great.

Such a childish way of thinking!

I treated the idea of baby as if it were an accessory. Something super cute to look at, but I never really stopped to think that it would have been a living thing that depended on me for everything.

Perhaps that's why I never got one.

After I had sex the first couple of times with one guy, I jumped to multiple guys. I figured that If I could get in a stable relationship with one, we could have sex often and that's how I would get my baby.

Well, the relationship parts never came through, so I spent most of that time just having sex with random guys.

Such emotionless sex.

I didn't feel anything. It was more for them than it was for me. Perhaps that's how I've managed to stay celibate for so long, I've never had sex with feeling.

It was always a sense of duty.

Right Back

It's saddens me to say that I never wanted to love my nephew. I wanted to reject him at every turn. Look him in the eye and have no feelings for him whatsoever.

I never wanted to love him.

Never.

Ever.

But as life goes, that was not the case. Once he came into this world, I knew there was nothing alive that could keep me out of his life. His tiny little hands and feet, with big brown eyes.

He was such a beautiful boy.

I remember the first time I held him. I'd had a long day and we were running around like crazy trying to get everything together so that they could come home.

I was so happy.

My little baby.

Our bond only got stronger as he got older. My sister and I moved into our first apartment together after only having a job at Popeye's for a little over a month. It's sad to say that not long after we signed our contract, we were fired and unemployed.

We only had that apartment for a month, but in that month, we got to experience a little of what adulthood had in store for us. There was almost freedom in there for a while.

When we went back to live with my parents in a small two-bedroom apartment, Rose and I were in constant close quarters. I would sometimes feel the jealousy, but only because my mother loved the baby so much.

I guess I shouldn't have been jealous of that. But it wasn't him. No. It channeled right back to my sister.

When she got an apartment on her own and a job working for a bar, she slowly started to change.

Once again, her life began to take off in ways mine just didn't.

She was able to buy her own car.

Move out.

Pay me to babysit.

It was like we were living our lives in reverse. She was the big sister showing ME how it should be done. My jealousy may have turned into inspiration then.

When she was required to work overnight, I would stay over and watch the baby. She would leave a few dollars for us to get something to eat before she went to work and we would play until he fell asleep.

There's something I miss about those days. Everything seemed so simple.

Eventually, she just asked me to move in with them, but she would still pay me to babysit—she even started leaving me with the car if I agreed to drop her off and pick her back up from work. She never even asked me to put gas back in the car.

There's no doubt in my mind that my sister loves me, that's for sure.

It's around that time that my nephew spent the most time with me. He'd started walking, talking and calling me NeNe. I would try and take him with me wherever I went.

He quickly became the Sun of my life to brighten up my day. He'll be called Ray.

I'm quite sure I fell in love with him.

When I think about how our relationship has progressed over the years, I cannot even imagine having the crazy thoughts that I did towards him. He became one of the single things holding me together when I wanted to give up so bad.

There was this one instance when I was having a tough day. I can't remember what was going on, but I felt as if my back was against the wall and I couldn't fight my way out.

I just wanted to quit everything I was working towards. I found myself sitting outside of my sister's apartment door on the top step crying in the dark. Then, the door opened behind me and this little boy comes up and puts his arm around me.

He told me not to be sad. That everything was going to be alright. Then, in true child-like fashion, he pointed up at the clouds and started to talk to me about the things he saw in them. The dinosaur on the skateboard, and the cowboy.

That moment, just like many of the other moments meant a lot to me. Here was a child who didn't see the failure that I saw in myself. He only saw the best in me. The NeNe who was always there.

This part really brings tears to my eyes. I've had to take several moments to pull myself together.

Now that he's older not much has changed about us. He will randomly text me sometimes and ask me to come pick him up for the weekend. He's in second grade now.

All of this feels like such a long time ago when really, this section only goes back to 2010. It's so interesting to see how things can change so much in a matter of years. Although he doesn't see himself as my baby anymore, because he's a big brother now, he's always going to be my chubby-faced, trouble-making, heart-stealing, baby.

Lights

It's the idea of me that I think people fall for.

No one ever cared to look at the person I was on the inside, and for a long time I was a magnet for people with severe insecurities.

I had so many of my own.

For years, I thought I was unattractive because I was obese. Never really realizing that it didn't matter is I was fat, had a peg leg, an eyepatch and a parrot on my shoulder, I still had one thing—a vagina.

The fact that I just so happened to be pretty was just a luxury. Meant that they could keep the lights on.

I took a personality test one time as an assignment for a psychology class that was creepily accurate. It said that I take qualities from people that I presume to be cool and absorb them into myself. So much of my life was spent perfecting that method.

I may have had a person for everything. Figuring that eventually I would be the complete package and no one would be able to resist me.

There was: charm, humor, confidence, charisma, and sarcasm, just to name a few of the things I leeched from people.

I remember my supply of confidence. It was this girl I'd met my first year of art school that was just ugly on the outside and inside.

I'm not just being malicious either. The girl was ugly. Even more than the fact that she was not an attractive woman was that she felt as though she could be unpleasant and obnoxious at the same time. But she was confident. So extremely confident, that you couldn't really tell her anything.

That was the thing that I needed. I fed off that confidence because she forced me to try and outdo her. To do that though, I had to be confident in my ability to get the job done. When I look back on it now, I was harnessing the wrong kind of confidence from her, because it wasn't very productive.

Or maybe I just didn't know what to do with all my newfound self-assurance and squandered it.

Who knows.

In either case, the only thing I used that confidence for was to score dates—and by dates, I just mean one-night-stands.

I first started sapping her confidence during our first semester. We had one class together, along with this one guy, John, whom she stated that she thought was attractive.

I didn't see him that way at first. He was a little sloppy, and unshaved, had this homeless type look to him, but he didn't stink.

It was never my intention on being anything with John than just a classmate, but one day he needed a ride home from school. Being the charitable person that I am, I decided to take him home. Plus, my mother was being more lenient with the car.

When we got to his apartment complex, he invited me up. I wasn't thinking anything of it at first. He offered me something to drink, and told me he was staying with a roommate.

There was no furniture in the house. Not even a chair. Just a computer desk and computer. Just the fact that he had an apartment was almost enough for me.

Low-hanging fruit, I tell you.

He had a bed too, which he wasn't shy about showing me. He flirted for a little bit, told me how beautiful I was. Said he'd been wanting to get to know me for a while now.

At this point, Kandace hadn't become my confidence supply yet, and I sort of just viewed her as a friend. That being the case, I told him that she had a thing for him and that I couldn't cross that line.

He said he understood.

But I was just more attractive than she was.

I didn't want to have sex with him either, but I did give him oral that day.

It seems so strange to me now how free and careless I was.

That was the first part of the day anyways, because we both had class later that night. As it would happen, Kandace was still on campus as well, and when I ran into her, I told her that I'd talked to John and told him that she was interested in getting to know him. Of course, I left out the part about me giving him top, because I still didn't really want to be with him.

What I thought was going to be a good thing, ended up just blowing up in my face, and from then on, I no longer considered her a friend. She told me I should have kept my mouth shut.

Well, after class, he invited me over to his house again and well, we went ahead and went for the real thing.

Several times.

I didn't even go home that night, and my mother was equal parts worried and frustrated because of it. Plus, it didn't help that my phone died and I didn't have a charger.

That ride home in the morning was worrisome.

My John phase didn't last very long, we had sex consistently for a few months. We agreed at first that we were just "having fun."

He didn't have a job; his mom was paying for everything and I would take him out to his hometown that was about 90 minutes away so that he could borrow drug money from his 100-year-old grandmother.

Naturally, the more we hung out, the more I cared less and less about those red flags. Because it was fun at first. It wasn't long before I became obsessive and jealous. When there was nothing to be jealous of. I was Queen of Overreacting.

I went over to his apartment one day in-between classes, and there was a woman coming down the stairs. My brain immediately told me they had sex.

I was having none of it.

What we had self-destructed so fast.

I'm sure it was for the best.

Wasn't long after that, Kandace had found a new flame. This one was attractive in every way. He was funny, fit, tall, and personable.

When he entered the picture, I was over John and I was now in full leech-mode of Kandace's confidence. I had to have him too. So, I dove in for the kill.

Like they all seemed to do, Marc took the bait. I was bold enough this time to flaunt my relationship with Marc in front of Kandace, while I'm sure he was trying to keep it a secret.

He was a medal.

I never had sex with him though, but I did get him to end their relationship. I'm sure he had a game going of his own, but in either case, I was playing my own mind games.

I was winning.

Two for two.

Once whatever Marc had going on no longer held my attention, I was on to putting targets on other backs.

Friend Request

Up to this point I've been exceptionally open. I've made it through some very difficult topics about my life, and the things in my past that I've never quite come forward and told anyone before. So, why does my stomach hurt when it comes to this?

To him.

I think I'm still getting over the influence that he's had over my life for such a long time. The crazy part is that everyone told me that something wasn't right about it. But you know how it is when you feel in every part of your being that you can be the change for another person.

You can make them change for you.

Well, I felt myself right on into a Narcissistic Abusive relationship—and I use the word relationship loosely. Everything was TAKE-TAKE. I was the one that was always giving. If he did give anything it was like a trinket just to keep me dangling on the end of his fish hook.

Welcome to present day.

I think I've had enough of talking about the past for a moment, and I've circled around the topic of this man for a while now. Partly trying to build the words in which to describe the things that he did to me.

Where should I even start?

From the top, obviously.

I wish I had never met him. I did this to myself. Remember when I said that it was largely due to the development of my own sense of arrogance? Yeah, well, I'll explain how.

Winston found his way into my life at a time when I was doing whatever I wanted too—which mainly included having sex for fun and pretending that I was someone that I was not.

When I was twenty-years-old, my mother had enough of me sitting around the house without a job and trying to finish a book that never seemed to be getting anywhere, and she gave me an ultimatum: get a job or go to school. She told me that most of my friends from high school had graduated already and were attending college. I should jump on the ship before it sails. If not, I would have to start working and pulling my own weight. I wasn't doing anything with my life. However, part of the school deal was that if I enrolled in college, she would support me through school.

So, seeing as I didn't want to work, and all my friends were in college, I decided to try out some colleges on my own. Realizing that she should take her own advice, my mother went out and enrolled herself into an Art Institute school. I figured it would be easier to get to school if I went with her, and it beat riding a bus, so I joined her at the same school.

We were in different programs though. She did Interior Design, while I signed up for Graphic Design. I must admit that at first learning design was the coolest thing, and the whole college experience was pretty great, even though I was on campus with my mother.

All college did was expand my reach, and it wasn't long after the first quarter that I was humping. The "school" was just the bottom floor of an office building and only had about ten or so classrooms and a photography studio. It was like a small town—everyone pretty much knew everyone.

Most of the guys there were white or some other ethnicity, and undoubtedly were rejects for most of their life. Some of them looked like their parents had given them the same ultimatum mine did and forced them to leave their nerd cave. It didn't take me long to figure out that I was able to charm pretty much anyone I wanted. So, I slept around. I flirted a lot.

There was this one guy though, his name was Peter, I thought he was everything. I may have heard through the grapevine that he was Cambodian. Either way, I wanted to be with him. Now, my confidence failed when it came to him because I was insecure about going after things I really wanted.

I had been used to getting the crumbs, I was apprehensive about going for the meat. But, I had a plan. I remember adding him as a friend on Facebook and liking a few of his pictures. Particularly, there was one that was okay, but nothing special—I could obviously tell that it had been taken with a decent camera—so I inquired about it. Complimented the picture just trying to make conversation. He told me that his friend did it and that if I wanted some pictures done, I should talk to him, since he went to the school too.

The moment I sent that friend request I was already on the path to destruction. My plan was to befriend the friend, Winston, to get him to put me in with his friend, Peter. Seems simple enough, right?

The descent to Hell was slow.

It didn't happen all at once.

It started with casual conversation. We would talk about setting up a photoshoot but he would take week-long intervals between messages, so it made it difficult to keep up with anything. It was right when I was about to throw in the towel that Satan sent him in for the kill.

One day he called me unexpectedly, and we talked for hours. The kind of talking where I paced around the house, laughing and really enjoying the conversation.

It went from there to texting back and forth every day.

He had made it known to me that he had a girlfriend, who also went to the school, but they were on a rough patch. I noticed he went from calling her his girlfriend to his ex in about a couple of weeks.

Gah! Everything makes so much sense.

Anyways, after about two months, I completely forgotten about Peter and was really interested in starting something with Winston. He was funny, charming, and spoke my language—sarcasm.

I thought we were going to be great.

I didn't see what he was doing to me.

My family noticed it first. I slowly started to change—and not for the better. I would enter these serious bouts of depression, not want to leave the house until he called and told me to meet him somewhere.

I spent all day and all night on the phone with him, and if we weren't on the phone, I was waiting by the phone for him to call. Which he did. Everyday. If he called and I didn't answer, or call him back within a reasonable amount of time, he made me feel like crap about it.

Soon, I was buying him expensive gifts, really trying to win his affection. He made sure the pressure was always on for me to really make him commit to me. Often, he would bring up Andrea like some sort of punishment. Which is unfair to her, because I don't even think she knew. Perhaps she's never seen this side of him, and may tell you that everything I'm saying is a downright lie. But deep down, I'm sure she knows. I'm sure she's felt it too. The evil within him.

He treated everything I did as if it were wrong. I had to spend so much time lifting his ego. Reminding him what a great person he is, how his photography work is unsurpassed, and that one day he will be great.

Meanwhile, he's making me feel like I should live my life to please him. He would often tell me in "jest" that if he were not in my life, it would not be worth living; so for a long time, I felt that way.

I felt like if we ever stopped talking, I wouldn't know how to move on—the pain would just be too great to bear.

Do you know we never bumped middles?

Another one of his bait tactics, because he knew that I wanted too so badly. He told me that I should stop having sex because when I finally find someone, I don't want to have too many miles.

I listened. It was logical. He said it's the same thing that he was doing. Trying to abstain from sex so that he didn't become a slave to his body.

I respected that.

We were never committed to each other. At least, he wasn't committed to me. In fact, for the length of our time together, we were never known as anything besides friends.

I stopped having sex. I waited for him. Except on a few occasions when I was manipulated into giving him oral.

Maybe that makes me a weak-minded girl. Perhaps it's not his fault.

You believe what you want. Like I said, I'm going to be honest, because I have no reason to lie.

Perhaps I should mention that his father is a preacher. I think it has a lot to do with why he turned out the way he did. If I have the story correct—and I think I do—he's the only one in his family that didn't exactly do anything great with their life. His sister has found success as a singer, and his brother has found an equal, if not greater, amount of success somewhere in Corporate America. Meanwhile, he has trouble holding on to a job.

He did finish college though, and it's easier for me to look back on the situation now from an objective standpoint and see just where the projection was rooted.

He projected all his failures, insecurities, and fears on me. But I was there the whole time to suck it right up. To absorb it all into myself, continuing to dig myself deeper into a depression that I have never known.

I wanted so badly to please him. To make him see that if he would choose me, it would be the best decision he could make. We could grow together, learn together. Everything would be alright, I just had to show him.

Prove to him that I'm the woman he needs.

Yet, time and time again, he would choose another woman. He would talk about these other girls to my face saying things that he liked about them so that I could absorb that into my personality.

I continuously sucked it all up.

There were so many girls over the years, and he would always say that I was the lucky one. It was me who kept moving on to the next round.

But I never went anywhere.

It was one giant merry-go-round that I couldn't get out of to save my life.

The thing that got me the most was that we continued to make memories, we tried new places together, went shopping, rode around the town, and to everyone else, we honestly looked like a couple. But he was sure to draw that line firmly in the sand when it was just us.

Us.

Humph.

There never was any **US**.

JUST HIM.

IT WAS <u>ALWAYS</u> JUST HIM.

I'm sorry, I didn't think I would still be angry, I found myself really pounding the crap out of my keyboard. Yeah, I must be really upset.

That's how I know I'm doing to right thing.

I'm getting all of this out in the open so that I can not only hear the words as they play like a broken record in my brain, but see them with my eyes.

As confirmation.

These things happened to me.

But look at me right now.

Breathing.

Taking one breath after the next, as if I haven't gone through a few storms in such a short lifespan.

For Myself

The dynamic started to shift a lot when I moved out of my parents' house and into my own apartment. I was about to graduate college after having to start over when I decided I no longer wanted a career in graphic design.

That's one year of my life I will never get back.

Anyways, I remember sitting in my living room trying to set up my television stand and on the phone with him when he told me he loved me.

Just a straight-up, vanilla, "I love you."

I thought this was the moment that was about to change my life. We were finally making gains in our relationship and he was ready to move forward.

Well, if not knowing you're attractive is a bag of cats, this was a jar of pythons.

Two days later, he told me that he regretted he'd even said anything at all, and would take it back if he could.

Well, I cried.

My spirit was so crushed, I think I spent the next couple of days in the house, not wanting to go anywhere or talk to anyone. I even let his calls go to voicemail.

I was just not in a good state of mind.

When I finally came out of my funk, I realized that I needed to do better. That after five years of being in a continuous loop with him, we weren't going anywhere. So, I cut him off for a while. Didn't respond to any of his messages, didn't call. That's not to say that I didn't think about him every.single.day, but I did hold off until he would call me.

Then, before you know it, I was right back in the loop. As I think about it all now, it just seems so depressing.

I was miserable.

But it was masked with happy moments and little acts of kindness he would do so that I didn't see what was really going on.

He needed me.

I was his supply for so long.

My career as a teacher was beginning to take off towards the finally cycle of our relationship. Because work kept me so occupied, I couldn't devote as much time to him and his needs anymore. I was also becoming increasingly weary of carrying the load he had given me to bear.

Let's reenter Andrea into the scene who was more of a pawn to get me jealous than she was anything else. He started to confess his undying love for her. Suddenly, she was the moon of his life and he didn't want to be with anyone else besides her.

See, I would have believed that.

Would have.

Except for the last time that I saw him in person, we had spent the whole day together. It had gotten late, and I realized that I should be heading home, when he told me I didn't have to leave. I could stay the night.

Well, for a few reasons, that was the biggest mistake I've made concerning my faith in a long time. If I haven't mentioned it to this point, I've been celibate for almost six years now, and he knew that.

It was his idea from the beginning. On this night, he enticed me. Seduced me.

I practically begged him.

But, again he wanted to use himself as bait. The truth of the matter is that he felt me slipping away. He knew that if he didn't do something drastic to keep me dangling there on his hook, he would lose me.

For good this time.

No. We didn't have sex.

But he touched me. Tenderly.

Grabbed two handfuls of my breasts and sat in front of me naked in the dark.

I don't like to think about it. It's one of the more recent memories I have of him.

The very thing that he hoped would make me stay, was the very thing that validated my decision to let it all go. To finally drop the anchor that I had been holding on to for him.

He finally pushed me away.

When I left his house the next morning, I felt the most worthless I've ever felt. It was as if everything that I had been working so hard towards was a complete failure.

I had no confidence.

No self-love.

I was willing to throw it all away for him. Only for him to turn it around and throw it back into my face. Like a spit in the eye. I realized during my hour drive home, that I couldn't allow that to happen again. I had to be stronger.

For myself.

That was the lesson in all of this for me. I had to learn how to push through the concrete, no matter how tough it may be.

At the end of it all, I wrote him a letter that I never sent. Although it was addressed to him, I never actually intended on sending it. I don't even think I wanted him to see it. But it explained so much about how I was feeling.

Dear Winston,

I held on as long as I could, despite how much it hurt me. You made sure I hurt. Everything you said. Everything you did. You never cared about anyone but yourself.

I was your narcissistic supply, and you drained me dry.

I was confused without knowing why.

Couldn't sleep at night, so I'd stay up and cry.

You never laid a hand on me, but somehow I would be in physical pain if I thought of my life without you in it. My chest would tighten. Breathing became heavy. Tears would spill like water over a levee.

But you knew exactly what you were doing, didn't you? The whole time.

Taking everything you could until there was nothing left, so you'd leave for awhile and let me restock. Then, the cycle would continue. I was the Diamond mine and you were the miner. You did your best to strip my inner strength so that I would succumb to whatever you wanted.

But you failed.

My strength doesn't come from me. God is my strength (Exodus 15:2). My shield (Psalms 28:7). You couldn't have it. I pleaded in tears to my Father to show me who you really are. Reveal the monster in you. The person you do your best to hide.

My Father took the veil off.

I saw everything clearly for the first time.

I knew cutting myself away from you suddenly wouldn't help me heal. It would only leave me with so many questions. So, I weaned myself. I played your game. Only this time, I could see your hand. Anticipate every move. I cut off your supply, leading you to believe that our separation was your idea, when in truth, I never wanted to speak to you again.

Oddly, I don't have any room in my heart to hate you, and for so long, this old heart of mine condemned me. Deceived me. Until finally I found comfort (1John 3:19,20).

This isn't to try and make you feel bad.

You're forced to live in an endless loop.

A hole.

A void you'll never fill.

That's why you project it on to others. I was in that place with you. It's so empty down there. For your crimes, that's punishment enough. My calling is higher; it was time for me to come out of it. Maybe someday you will too.

I'm forgiving you. I'm forgetting you.

I just wanted to leave this letter here, all about the one person you care about most in this world. You.

No Longer Yours,

Myunique

A Heartbeat

Congratulations!

You made it all the way here.

Up to this point, I've just been relaying the facts. Picking out some stories and sorting them out in a logical way. Expressing how I feel or how I felt.

I omitted the spiritual side of those things because I wanted to get to this point right here.

This point of acceptance.

You had to take the journey with me, and I hope I haven't lost you. Of course, if you're still reading, you may as well go ahead and stick it out to the end.

Now, I'm going to talk to you as a woman.

A spiritual woman.

The woman that was delivered from so many situations that could have gone from bad to worse in a heartbeat.

I mentioned that my mother studied and raised us as Jehovah's Witnesses from the time that I was about nine, up to my teen years. I was going through so much crap in my own head that I couldn't let anyone else in.

I was so shut off.

But, I did my studies. I went to all the meetings like I didn't have a choice and I even went out from door-to-door in the preaching ministry

It didn't make sense to me then.

For a long time, I thought I wanted to get baptized because it was like a rite of passage kind of thing. The friends that I could have had started getting baptized and there I was, left out again.

Everything that I was doing wasn't for God's Glory, it was for my own. I was still out to prove that I mattered. That I couldn't just be thrown by the wayside and forgotten about for the rest of my life.

I was going to do something that counted.

Even in my lackluster effort, my sister received all of the recognition. They thought she was going to do great things, and me, well, I would just end up in a ditch somewhere.

That's no joke either.

Years later, someone plainly told me they thought I would end up in a ditch.

I don't think she was even saying it to be malicious. But I do think her speech was reckless.

Maybe as a teenager I was just that heedless that it would led them to assume that of me. Like I didn't take anything seriously and so I was probably better off dead.

It's a good thing that God is the ultimate judge.

When I look at my story now, I think it's harder for me to feel sorry for myself. I don't possess that same sense of self-pity that I held on to for so long.

No more woe-is-me.

Because in my heart I believe that there was a greater purpose for me to experience those things. There's a young lady out there right now that is going through what I went through—maybe even to more extremes.

I want to talk to her.

If she's anything like I was, she probably wouldn't want to hear it from someone who doesn't understand.

But I do.

I understand the broken pieces she tries so hard to mend together but with every passing day the vase that is her heart gets shattered all over again.

I understand being stuck in a loop that never seems to end because she feels her voice will never be heard, and if they hear it, they still wouldn't care.

For so many years, I was that girl.

It's easy for people to talk about things that they don't understand. Say you should get over it, and start healing. But do they ever really tell you how? Or what healing even looks like? So, you've done what I did and buried it all. Just so you can have the semblance of a normal life—because it doesn't hurt if you can't remember it.

But you do remember.

It affects everything you do, and every decision that you make. I realized that I needed to do this a few months ago when I found myself losing my marbles in the back of a squad car—and the officers were only giving me a ride from the side of the freeway after my car had stalled. Once the back door closed and I realized that it had no handles, an anxiety attack

The panic attacks had started to become increasingly frequent. I would never have guessed that simple things would trigger me. Granted, I was trying to deal with stressful situations.

The news that I was insane spread so fast throughout my family, and everyone needed to know if I was alright.

I remember sitting down with my aunt and really having a heart to heart with her until she told me some things that I not only did not want to hear, but that I felt were just completely off base and ludicrous. She was not the only one that felt that way though.

The People

I hold myself to a lot higher esteem these days. For instance, I've realized that both inside and out, I'm quite attractive. I ran a count on how many times I've used that word and it came back nine separate times.

I thought I used it more than that.

Even more than my attractiveness, I talk a lot about acceptance. Coming to terms with a few things. It's important to know that there are both healthy and unhealthy forms of acceptance.

Accepting things that you can't change—healthy.

Accepting your feelings of worthlessness—unhealthy.

Can you see the difference?

Whatever challenges you are facing or have faced in life, you are going to have to accept them.

That's the only way you're going to be able to move on.

Truly move one.

Once you have found the strength within yourself to let things go for you, and not because someone else told you too, you're going to feel a lot better.

I promise.

I had to bring myself here.

Drag myself!

Because it was not easy.

None of it was easy. Even more so since they were still affecting decisions in my life. Talking about this and putting it all down meant that these were not just elaborate stories I made up in my brain to pass the time. *They wanted me to believe that for so long.*

I admitted to myself–and strangers–that these things happened to ME. And you know what? That's okay! I believe I have purpose. I believe <u>YOU</u> have purpose.

I've gone from being a girl with a story to tell to having: *Purpose*. Not just *Passion*.

While writing is my passion, there is a purpose to it. I can write my story in a way that hopefully you can understand, because life is complicated enough already.

People will still only see what you show.

They'll hear what they want to hear.

But don't let that stop you from speaking.

Don't let it hinder you from showing the world just how amazing you are. It's time for the little girl inside all of us to be free.

Find a way to mend the pieces.

If you're spiritual, I challenge you to go in prayer, be specific, ask, plead and beg for the strength to overcome.

If you're not, spend some time in meditation, reflect on some of the things that have led you to your current situation.

That's not me telling you what to do.

I think one of the key things is to never draw away from people. Even though being a recluse may seem like the answer, a lot of times it has the opposite effect on us and we become more vulnerable.

Means the darkness only looms.

I'm not one of those people that's going to tell you to just get over it either. Believe me. I've had so many of those types of people in my life. What I am going to tell you is to be strong.

Be patient.

Even though things may not be how you want them to be right now, things can quickly change.

In my case, although I've been broken for a while, ultimately it was never up to me to put the pieces back together.

It was my God.

That's why I don't see anything that I've done as any accomplishment of my own. It took Him to show me that I was worth more than what I was choosing to accept in my life.

The people.

The false friends.

Even family.

I came to realize that at any time, anyone can let you down. You're going to need an anchor.

No, not the type of anchor that's going to hinder you from moving, and keep you planted in one place. But, the kind of anchor that's going to ground you when the waters are choppy. When you find yourself out there getting tossed around and crushed underneath tremendous pressure.

That's what God has been for me.

My strength.

My comfort.

My friend.

He holds his hands out to you too.

I'm here to tell you not to give up. That just like me, your story isn't over yet. You still have time to shine and be great.

But, I also don't want you to just take my word for it.

Take God's word.

Put it into your heart and allow him to speak to you. You'll have to open your eyes to see it for yourself though.

A lot of times, the things He does for us will go unacknowledged because we simply lack the foresight to see them as anything other than a loving Father looking out for His wayward children.

That's okay.

He understands, and to me, that's the beauty of it all.

The mere fact that He gave us freewill to begin with. I want to share some scriptures that have helped me, and not only just share them, but also explain what they mean to me and what they can mean to you.

Philippians 4:13

"For all things, I have the strength through the one who gives me power."

The Takeaway: If you make the source of your power the Almighty, you will be able to overcome just about anything. Because He will never let you down. Come what may. Seems simple enough, but sometimes it's harder to do than you may realize. A lot of times, we want to do things ourselves. To say that we overcame it through the skin on our teeth, and that may work for a while. But don't you get tired? Do situations eventually just seem too hard to bear anymore? Let God put that power back into your life. Draw your strength from Him.

1 Peter 5:10

"But after you have suffered a little while, the God of all undeserved kindness will himself finish your training. He will make you firm, he will make you strong, he will firmly ground you."

The Takeaway: All the pain and the suffering that you are currently undergoing is only going to last for a little while! Even if you feel like it's been forever and there's no way that you can carry on; remember this scripture. Because God's kindness is extremely undeserved, and He says that HE HIMSELF will make you firm! not that He's going to put someone in your life to do it for you, but that He will make the time for you to be set straight. How loving is that? This is one of my favorite scriptures because of the simple promise that everything that I'm going through in life is just a part of my training. Meant to make me a better, more efficient, minister and person.

Colossians 3:23

> "Whatever you are doing, work at it whole-souled as for Jehovah, and not for men."

<u>The Takeaway</u>: This is another one of those scriptures that seems simple, until it's not. Sometimes, we can get caught up into thinking that no one cares or it doesn't really matter what we are doing, so we may do it halfheartedly, or begrudgingly. This can be at work, at school, or any avenue of our life where it just doesn't seem worth it to put forth any extra effort. The key thing to remember is that God watches. He knows when we are giving our best. So, it's up to us to exercise good judgement in all areas of life.

Psalms 61:8

> "Then I will sing praises to your name forever, as I pay my vows day after day."

The Takeaway: One of the biggest things for me was finding out that God had a name when I was about six years old. It wasn't because anyone had told me His name either, I just so happened to be eavesdropping on a bible study my mother was having and overheard the lady say the name. I don't think that I would have ever imagined from that moment I would come to know the One behind that name and develop a relationship with him. Although rocky at first. I couldn't have possibly grasped the idea that He would be the One stand by me when my world was crumbling down. Knowing, and understanding, that His name was one of the essential things in building that relationship. Drawing close to him. After all, the scripture in James 4:8 tells us: "Draw close to God, and he will draw close to you." It doesn't mean that you must be perfect–because let's face it, you're not–but the simple fact that you are willing to try is a step in the right direction.

Psalms 28:7

"Jehovah is my strength and my shield. In him my heart trusts. I have received his help, and my heart rejoices, so I will praise him with my song."

The Takeaway: You may have noticed that I also quoted this scripture in my letter to Winston. That's because I really believe this with my whole heart.

When no one else was there for me, God was. He helped me when I had given up on myself and I trust in everything He has done in my life so far. I can never go wrong if I keep allowing myself to stay behind his shield and direct my steps.

Not Over Yet

I should finish the way I started: with my mother, with Winston, or with coming to terms with situations in life that I cannot change.

But I really don't want to.

I'm ready to close this part of my life and continue to develop the woman that I'm becoming. I can no longer allow myself to hold on to things that are only there to keep me down. One of those bad anchors I spoke about earlier.

My mother was one of the first to read this in its early stages. I'll say that she isn't the person she was all those years ago. We've both grown a lot and I've accepted enough to just let it go.

I realize now what I couldn't possibly have grasped years ago that she was a broken woman too. But I can't tell her story. I can only relate how her demons spread down to me—how they tried to keep me down in that broken place full of resentment and despair.

If it's not obvious by now, I became a minister—something I'm very proud of.

On October 19, 2014 I was baptized as one of Jehovah's Witnesses, much to the dismay of my sister and other relatives. My sister thought that I only did it because I wanted to live up to some ideal that my mother and grandmother had for me. As if I had been pressured into taking the dip.

I mentioned awhile back that when I was a teenager getting baptized was like a rite of passage kind of thing—everyone was doing it.

Sure, I wanted to. But there was just something standing in the way for me to make it to the pool. To be baptized, you have to answer a series of questions and depending on your answers, they can either suggest you study a little more, or approve you for baptism.

I never made it to the questions.

Granted, I could have given all the right answers, but that still wouldn't have changed where my heart was. It just wasn't time. I had more things to experience. Bigger lessons to learn. God knew that I wasn't doing it for the right reasons then.

I think that people have their own misconceptions about Jehovah's Witnesses and while I never disagreed with any of the teachings, I hadn't really experienced anything outside of it either. I was always taught that sex before marriage is bad. Anything that had to do with magic or the supernatural is bad. Teaching people about God, Jesus and the kingdom is good.

The many years I spent out doing my own thing never really brought me any sense of accomplishment. I had no real joy. If anything, I was apathetic. Then, there was always that lingering guilt that would wash over me if I thought about it too long.

So, I just stopped thinking.

I allowed myself to be taken advantage of, somehow gaining this odd idea that eventually I would find that missing piece.

You want to know what broke me?

What jolted me awake so forcefully that my spirit felt as if it were on fire?

I saw an old picture of myself at a Christian gathering. It was an off-guard shot that caught me sitting there laughing and having a good time with people who I can say now were trying to help me.

My eyes were swimming with tears as I stared at it. Remembering the good times that I had and how I actually enjoyed being out telling people about God.

It didn't just stop there though. The following weekend there was a three-day convention where we all gathered to listen to sermons and learn more effective ways of teaching and how to improve our quality of life.

I FELT God's spirit talking to me all three of those days. I can't remember how many times I cried.

On the final day, there was just a voice that said it was time to come back. To make things right so that I could teach again.

Feel again.

I'll never forget that moment.

Since I was staying with my grandmother for that weekend, I'd went back to her house only to realize that I had left something somewhere else. My grandmother just told me to go get it but to hurry back.

The whole ride there I was mostly silent while the songs played. I didn't really know any of them, but I appreciated the melodies nonetheless. Once I was on the way back however, there was this one song that I did know play across the speaker.

Christian Dedication.

I still tear up when I hear that song.

Anyways, when that song came on that night, I was in a puddle of tears flying down the freeway, barely holding it together.

I told God I needed help. I could no longer go on living on my own, and doing things my way. My decisions had led me to so many failures.

I wish I can say that everything changed overnight. That when I woke up, my whole life was cleaned up and I was no longer suffering from depression—I really wish I could.

But something did change.

I saw that purpose come back to life. I had more reason that I ever had to get back up on the horse and keep riding.

Since my sister still had demons of her own to clean out of her life, and her lifestyle wasn't super conducive to the changes I needed to make, I decided to go back home and live with my mother.

Would you know that about a day later, my stepfather gave me a piece of paper with a lady's name and phone number on it? He said that she had come by and wanted me to give her a call.

I held on to that number for a while before calling and finding out what the lady wanted—she was a Jehovah's Witness.

Go figure, right?

I took that as the sign I needed that it was finally time to get up, resume my studies, and God would be there to continue guiding me.

Although, initially, it was at Winston's behest that I stop having sex, it ended up being the best decision I'd made. It made it easier for me to make the other adjustment I needed to make in my life.

A year later I was baptized.

Do you know what song played at my baptism?

That's right, *Christian Dedication*.

I'm all for letting people believe what they believe and worship whatever God they want to. You'll never catch me throwing Bible's at people or debating on whether you should celebrate Christmas or not. Yet, in that same token, there isn't anything that anyone can tell me about the God I chose to believe in.

The God that revealed Himself to me, and called me to the course that I now take.

1 Peter 2:21

"In fact, to this course you were called, because even Christ suffered for you, leaving a model for you to follow his steps closely."

1 Peter 3:9

"For you were called to this course, so that you might inherit a blessing."

Maybe that makes me brainwashed? That's okay if you believe that. Doesn't make any never mind to me. It's interesting that by now, my mother has gone off on her own path and isn't a practicing JW anymore, and if you ask her, she has no problems telling you why.

She's still so broken.

Even though I can't say that I'm completely mended, I can tell you that I have peace and understanding. I found the glue that binds me together. The helping hand that hands me the pieces whenever I'm shattered all over the floor.

It wasn't Winston. It wasn't money. It wasn't even family.

It's always been Jehovah.

My prayer is that you find your glue too, and that every moment is filled with happiness and joy. *It's time for you to feel again.*

A Look Back in 2025

When I first wrote this book in 2018, I was still learning how to hold my own story without letting it crush me. I didn't have all the words, or all the confidence, or even all the clarity—but I had the courage to open old wounds and say, *This is what shaped me.* Back then, I was writing toward a future I didn't know would ever come. A future where I felt healed. A future where I felt seen. A future where I felt whole enough to stop shrinking in my own life.

Looking back now, I see a woman who was fighting her way toward that version of herself even when she didn't believe she deserved it.

So much life has unfolded since these pages were first printed. I became a wife, and later, I walked away from that marriage. That part of my journey changed me in ways I didn't expect. Love taught me tenderness. Separation taught me clarity. What I know now is that marriage is not the destination I once imagined. Peace is. Wholeness is. A love that grows from within me, before it ever grows beside me, is the only kind I'm willing to accept anymore.

And then—my greatest blessing arrived.

For years, tucked between the lines of this book, was the ache for a child I wasn't sure I'd ever have. I wrote about wanting to give my mother her first grandchild; I wrote about longing for someone to love who was mine. I didn't know it then, but my son was already written into my life long before he was born. In 2024, he came into this world on a palindrome day—4/24/24—perfect forward and backward, just like the way he completely rearranged my life and made it make sense both ways.

Becoming Cove's mother has softened me, strengthened me, and stretched me in ways that only love can. He is the answered prayer I didn't know how to ask out loud. Every day with him is a reminder that even broken hearts can grow new rooms.

And somewhere between motherhood and healing and learning myself all over again, another dream came to life: *Anywhere But Here*.

I will never forget the morning it went viral. Watching it climb Amazon's charts and hit Top Release in its category was surreal. For a long time, I had written in my own small corner of the world, hoping my voice mattered. That moment showed me that readers were actually finding me—finding my words—and holding onto them. It was a validation I didn't expect but will always be grateful for.

Looking back at this book now feels like opening a time capsule. These chapters capture the version of me who was piecing herself together one painful truth at a time. I honor her for telling her story before she knew how it would end, before she knew she'd become a mother, before she knew her words would travel further than her fear.

I'm not the woman who wrote this book in 2018. I'm stronger. Softer. Clearer. I've learned to protect my peace like it's sacred, because it is. I've learned that healing isn't something you arrive at—it's something you choose every day. And I've learned that the girl who felt invisible for so long grew up to become a woman who refuses to dim her own light ever again.

Thank you for returning to these pages with me, and for witnessing who I was and who I've become. I hope this edition reminds you that growth is not always loud. Sometimes it happens quietly, in the background, shaping you in ways you won't understand until you pause and look back.

The Parts I Never Said

(…a bonus)

There were things I didn't have the strength to put on the page the first time. Not because they weren't true, but because I didn't yet know how to tell the truth without bleeding all over it. Back then, healing felt like something other people got to claim. I was just trying to survive long enough to write anything down at all.

What I didn't say was how often I felt like I was standing outside my own life, watching a girl I didn't know carry burdens meant for grown people. I didn't say how lonely it was to become everyone's safe space when I didn't have one myself. I didn't say how much I internalized, how much I forgave, how much I swallowed just to keep the peace that never really belonged to me.

I didn't say how many times I wanted to disappear—not to die, but to stop hurting long enough to breathe without flinching. I didn't say that some scars only stopped aching when I became a mother and realized my heart had room for new beginnings after all. I didn't say how many years I spent shrinking, molding, performing, hoping someone would finally see me and tell me I wasn't too much or too little.

What I know now is that silence was survival, but it was never freedom.

The parts I never said were the parts that scared me: the anger, the grief, the resentment, the confusion, the dreams I tucked away because I didn't think they belonged to someone like me. I used to think speaking them out loud made me weak. But now I understand it took strength to hold them—and even more strength to let them go.

So here they are, softly laid down, after all this time.

I was hurting.

I was trying.

I was learning myself in slow, jagged pieces.

And I was worthy the whole time, even when I didn't believe it.

This is the truth behind the truth: Healing didn't come because I spoke everything—I didn't. Healing came because I finally stopped running from the parts I never said.

About Myunique

Myunique C. Green is an award-winning independent author and the founder of iWriteBooks Publishing. Known for her dynamic range, she writes psychological thrillers, Southern Gothic, fantasy, YA, romance, and more—always centering Black women and crafting stories that blend emotional depth with bold, imaginative storytelling. Her books have been featured in book clubs, libraries, and literary spaces across the country, supported by a dedicated readership and a rapidly expanding catalog.

Alongside her writing career, Myunique is a special education teacher, a mother, and a creative entrepreneur who produces multimedia projects, and original artwork that complement her stories. Her work is grounded in intention, community, and craft, and she continues to build new worlds that resonate with readers seeking powerful, character-driven fiction.

Made in the USA
Coppell, TX
20 December 2025

64703915R00101